Contemporary Perspectives in Data Mining

A volume in
Contemporary Perspectives on Data Mining
Kenneth D. Lawrence and Ronald K. Klimberg, *Series Editors*

Contemporary Perspectives in Data Mining

Volume 3

edited by

Kenneth D. Lawrence
New Jersey Institute of Technology

Ronald K. Klimberg
Saint Joseph's University

INFORMATION AGE PUBLISHING, INC.
Charlotte, NC • www.infoagepub.com

Library of Congress Cataloging-in-Publication Data

A CIP record for this book is available from the Library of Congress
http://www.loc.gov

ISBN: 978-1-64113-054-7 (Paperback)
       978-1-64113-055-4 (Hardcover)
       978-1-64113-056-1 (ebook)

CONTENTS

SECTION I

PREDICTIVE ANALYTICS

SECTION II

BUSINESS APPLICATIONS

SECTION III
TOPICS IN DATA MINING

SECTION I

PREDICTIVE ANALYTICS

CHAPTER 1

BOOTSTRAP AGGREGATION FOR NEURAL NETWORK FORECASTING OF SUPPLY CHAIN ORDER QUANTITY

Mark T. Leung[1] and Shaotao Pan
University of Texas at San Antonio

ABSTRACT

Order forecasting has long been an imperative issue in many outsourcing supply chains in the manufacturing sector. Although some of these supply chain relationships call for a long-term contractual agreement, order quantity is often influenced by economic conditions, market factors, and order fluctuations in similar or related items. Given this notion, a variety of models have been developed for the prediction of future order quantity placed by a supply chain partner. Among them, recent studies adopting artificial neural networks (ANNs) have found promising results to fulfill this planning purpose. An ANN has the capacity to perform nonlinear estimation without assumptions on linearity and underlying distribution form. In this study, we demonstrate how to apply the *bootstrap aggregation* (also commonly known as bagging) framework to neural network forecasting and, at the same time,

Contemporary Perspectives on Data Mining, Volume 3, pages 3–27
Copyright © 2018 by Information Age Publishing

to resolve some imperative issues related to the prediction of product order quantity in supply chain planning (such as data preprocessing and consolidation to product family). In addition, we explore how the number of bootstrap samples, which reflects the required level of computational burden, affects the performance of the neural network forecasts. Specifically, bootstrap samples are generated from the preprocessed supply chain order dataset according to standard bagging procedure. Each of these bootstrap samples is then applied to the in-sample training of different ANNs, yielding diverse series of out-of sample estimated changes in order quantities for blind testing. This entire empirical process is repeated with different numbers of bootstrap samples. Results are benchmarked with order quantity forecasts from corresponding ANNs of no bagging, conventional ARIMA, and random walk models. Our finding indicates that the bagging framework enhances the overall performance and creates more persistent accuracy in order forecasts over the long run. Moreover, improvement in performance due to bagging is significant, but varies across different neural network designs. It has also been found that the performance of forecasting with bagging follows the pattern of diminishing marginal return. In other words, performance improves at a decreasing rate with the increasing level of computation (the number of bootstraps). These conclusions hold for different network architectural designs although the impact of bagging enhancement is not uniform across different neural networks.

Supply chain management has been considered one of the essential functional areas in business over the past decades. It is especially critical to multinational corporations that have to coordinate material flows through a supply network involving global partnerships. Lack of coordination or synchronization among supply chain partners may create and propagate disruption from one partner to others due to mutual reliance/interdependence in countless numbers of operations such as production, inventory control, manpower planning, and more. Although the management of supply chain partners often takes into account planned activities (such as promotional events or temporary price cuts to induce forward buying) at downstream stages, unexpected outcomes or inaccuracy may still occur, resulting in an unwanted reduction in local if not systemwide profitability. Thus, it is important for upstream partners to generate reliable forecasts for order quantities expected to be placed by their immediate downstream partners. One major purpose of such forecasting task is to assist in advance planning of changeover in scheduling, labor assignment, etc. Another crucial purpose is to provide a validation of possible order forecasts previously furnished by a downstream partner (i.e., customer.) For example, an overseas manufacturer of components used in the production of electronic devices in the United States may want to estimate the quantities of certain major components to ensure that its expected future production plan aligns with the known reality. This is because the large order quantities, the long shipping distance, together with contractual logistical commitment within the supply chain may practically prohibit the overseas manufacturer from correcting an error in a timely fashion without negatively disrupting the downstream U.S. operations. In general, the higher the level of supply chain risk entailed, the more prominent is the role of supply chain order forecasting. Readers can refer to Chopra and Meindl (2016) for more detailed information regarding supply chain coordination, respective risk involved, and order forecasting.

Advancements in technology in the last two decades have revolutionized our way of conducting business forecasting. This allows us to perform more elaborated computation with a higher degree of accuracy. One such advancement is the adoption of artificial intelligence (AI) in statistical modeling and estimation. Among those numerous applications of AI in modeling is the use of artificial neural networks (ANNs) in the fields of operations, finance, marketing and many other business functional areas. Tkac and Verner (2016) provide a recent comprehensive review of ANN-oriented literature in business. Within this avenue of research, there exists numerous studies utilizing ANNs for supply chain or production management. Some examples in the industrial setting are found in Carbonneau, Laframboise, and Vahidov (2008); Thomassey (2010); Tsai and Hung (2016); Lau, Ho, and Zhao (2013); Weese, Martinze, Megahed, and Jones-Farmer (2016).

In our study, we focus on a two-stage supply chain environment where an upstream partner fulfills the production order of parts or components for a downstream partner (who is another manufacturer providing an additional value-added function). Based on the previous example mentioned, the overseas manufacturer is the upstream partner producing and shipping the components to the downstream partner (customer) for further processing or assembling of electronic devices in the United States. This relatively simple supply chain configuration lets us concentrate our attention on the primary research issues of this study: how to utilize or implement a neural network in supply chain order forecasting and how to improve its forecast performance.

Using ANN in supply chain order forecasting may embrace a number of implementation challenges in addition to an array of technical issues related to the training and proper selection of network models. For instance, patterns of changes in future order quantity may not be fully observable in existing historical data. This situation arises at the emergence of innovative product designs, new business and economic conditions, and special terms of supply chain relationships. Since the new information is not reflected in the training dataset, an ANN may not be able to generate a sensible forecast (i.e., a meaningful reaction when it is subject to an input vector of independent variables unseen before.) On the other hand, an adequate amount of data may not be available for network training. Low periodic frequency of ordering, short-term subcontracting status, and orders of nonstandardized items are some of the possible sources of data inadequacy. To address these problems, we propose the adoption of a bootstrap aggregation (bagging) framework in conjunction with neural network forecasting of supply chain order quantity. This resampling procedure should enhance the forecast quality while alleviating the spurious effect of relatively unstable or limited data on network training.

To create more generalized conclusions, two separate neural network architectural designs are used in the proposed bagging framework: *multilayer feed forward neural network* (MLFN) and *general regression neural network* (GRNN). They have been chosen because both architectural designs yield promising results in many business forecasting studies e.g., Claveria, Monte, and Torra (2015); Leung, Chen, and Mancha (2009); and Venkatesh, Ravi, Prinzie, & Van den Poel (2014). As they will describe in "Methodologies," these two network designs require different training paradigms and sets of parameters (hype-parameters) for learning. Comparisons of their performances over the five evaluation criteria measured in the experiment, as well as their relative improvement over corresponding bagging models, should generate additional insights into the practice.

In summary, the major purposes of the current study are: (a) to demonstrate how bagging is adapted and applied to neural network forecasting of supply chain order quantity; (b) to investigate the gain in forecast accuracy of different network models due to bagging and performances relative to ARIMA and random walk models; and (c) to explore the impact of the number of bootstrap samples on the quality of bagging enhancement.

This chapter is organized as follows. An abbreviated review of relevant literature is given in the next section. In "Methodologies," the primary methodologies used in the empirical investigation are described and their technical foundations are briefly explained. These include the two neural network designs—MLFN and GRNN—selected for examination in our study and the proposed bootstrap aggregation (bagging) framework for enhancement of neural network forecasting. Then, the supply chain order dataset and data preprocessing (transformation) applied to the forecasting analysis are documented in "Data and Empirical Experiment." Training of the neural networks and selection of the best model specification are also clarified. Further, the section details the procedure of embedding the MLFN and GRNN order forecasting into the proposed bagging framework. "Results and Discussion" reports the forecast performances of neural networks with and without the bagging enhancement. The results are also benchmarked against those of ARIMA and random walk models.

Subsequently, the impact of the number of bootstrap samples on the two ANNs' forecast quality is explored in the auxiliary experiment. The section also discusses the results and provides insights pertinent to our research problem. Conclusions as well as ideas for future extensions are given in "Conclusions."

LITERATURE REVIEW

Order Forecasting Especially Using Neural Networks

Forecasting the size of a future customer order plays an important role in inventory planning and control. Order quantity is sensitive to economic conditions and market influence. In a make-to-order environment, which is commonly seen in a supply chain, fulfillment of orders is followed by the scheduling of production orders. A much larger-than-expected error in the order forecast may lead to either a shortage or excessive inventory. Thus, to ensure a smooth material flow and to avoid a rise in inventory costs, many forecasting methods and techniques have been developed. Interested readers should check out Makridakis, Wheelwright, and Hyndman (1998) for methods in general forecasting or Chase (2013) for methods in demand order forecasting.

Exponential smoothing and regression analysis are universally accepted statistical methods that have been used for several decades in forecasting demand orders. In general, most smoothing models average out the previously observed demands in a decreasing exponential manner, and assign larger weights to more recent demands. On the other hand, regression models attempt to create a relationship between the demand and an array of exogenous and endogenous input variables. Through the model estimated from historical data, a future demand forecast can be projected from a given set of input variables. Readers can refer to Chase (2013); Leung, Quintana, and Chen (2009); Mabert (1978); and Quintana and Leung (2007) for a formal exposition of these traditional time series methods for order forecasting.

However, traditional time series methods may apply inaccurate functional form to independent and dependent variables (Hill, O'Connor, & Remus 1996). These misused relationships may be harmful for the model fitting process (1996). Also, many of these models are sensitive to outliers who can generate bias during the estimation of model (Iman & Conover, 1988). As for nonlinear relationships, it is usually hard for a traditional model to fit (see Makridakis et al., 1982, for a comparison of traditional times series methods). As a result, many recent studies have adopted artificial neural networks (ANNs), which have found promising results in industrial supply chain forecasting (e.g., Heravi, Osborn, & Birchenhall 2004). Basically, ANNs are models with high flexibility in such a way that they have the capability to model nonlinear relationships without explicitly specifying the assumptions of the forms of models and/or the underlying distributions of parameters (Hornik, Stinchcombe, & White 1989; White 1992).

Gutierreza, Solis, and Mukhopadhyay (2008) first proposed a study using ANN in forecasting lumpy demand. A three-layer MLFN (perceptron) is trained by a back-propagation algorithm. Based on overall *mean absolute percentage errors* (MAPSs), the neural network generally performs better than traditional methods, single exponential smoothing, Croston's method [1972], and Syntetos and Boylan's approximation [2005] in their forecasting experiment.

At the same time, Pour, Tabar, and Rahimzadeh (2008) developed a hybrid forecasting approach, with a *multilayered feed forward neural network* (MLFN) for forecasting lumpy demand. In their method, the MLFN is trained to forecast the occurrences of nonzero demands, and then a recursive method is applied to estimate the quantity of nonzero demand.

Leung, Quintana, and Chen (2009) proposed a two-stage forecasting approach. In the first stage, a smoothing model is applied to estimate the series of demand forecasts. In the second stage, a general regression neural network (GRNN) is subsequently used to forecast the resulting error (residual) function. In this manner, the originally forecasted demand in the first stage can be updated (improved) by reversing the estimated error from the second stage. This study also discusses the outperformance of GRNN relative to exponential smoothing models (simple exponential smoothing model, Holt's exponential smoothing model, Winter's exponential smoothing model, adaptive exponential smoothing model, and dynamic exponential smoothing model using Kalman filter). Besides, when coupled with each of these smoothing models in the first stage, the two-stage model is able to reduce the RMSE of corresponding single-stage counterpart.

In recent years, a handful of studies have incorporated ANNs into intermitted demand forecasting, e.g., Syntetos and Boylan (2005), Syntetos, Nikolopoulos, and Boylan (2010), and Teunter and Sani (2009). Usually the proposed ANN-driven models are compared against a number of benchmark models and show promising results. More recently, a bivariate ANN model was developed by Kourentzes (2013). This special forecasting model explicitly takes into account the interactions between demand and interdemand intervals. It found that the forecasts made by the bivariate ANN models are robust, even with a small in-sample dataset for training.

Bagging as a Variance Reduction Method

Bootstrap aggregating (bagging) was introduced by Breiman (1996) as a method for variance reduction in estimation. He proposed using bootstrap samples resampled (with replacement) from a dataset to generate multiple dissimilar predictors, which are then aggregated to form the bagging predictor. He postulated that this aggregation procedure should lead to a more stable and reliable predictor with a higher degree of estimation accuracy. When the dataset used for estimation is large and in higher dimensions, the bagging method becomes especially useful (Büchlmann & Yu, 2002). Breiman

(1996) also pointed out that bagging can significantly improve the mean squared error (MSE) for unstable data (i.e., a data set in which small changes in input variables can lead to a large change in the predicted variable). Additional theoretical analyses were subsequently furnished by Friedman and Hall (2007), Buja and Stuetzle (2000), and Büchlmann and Yu (2002). Moreover, Büchlmann introduced a technique called *subagging* (subsample aggregating) to reduce the computational complexity, while demonstrating approximately the same accuracy as the conventional bagging method.

Originally, bagging was applied to regression trees and classification trees (Breiman 1996). Bagging can also be used for Bayesian prediction (Clyde & Lee, 2001) or tree-based ranking prediction (Clémençon & Vayatis, 2009). The empirical results agreed with the notion that bagging can improve the prediction by reducing the variance inherent to estimation from unstable or ill-fitting data. In terms of ANN, the majority of prior research focused on how to identify the most accurate model for a specific application. This single-model strategy may be inaccurate or even misleading. In light of this, Krogh and Vedelsby (1995) proposed an ensemble algorithm to effectively aggregate ANNs by bagging. Following their study, many recent investigations have been made to improve the accuracy of aggregated ANNs (such as Chandra & Yao, 2006; Chen & Yu, 2007; West, Dellana, & Qian, 2005; Zhou, Wu, & Tang, 2002). A large number of literatures have demonstrated that ensembles of many ANNs model could reduce the error rate (e.g., Breiman 1996; Breiman 1999; Dietterich 2000; Khwaja, Naeem, Anpalagan, Venetsanopoulos, & Venkatesh, 2015).

Over the last 10 years, using ensembles has been accepted more or less as an unwritten standard for ANN forecasting, which could reduce the uncertainties or potential errors from sampling or modeling (Zhou, Wu & Tang, 2002). The improvement in accuracy, however, is often associated with how the forecasting models are combined (Stock & Watson, 2006). Conventionally, mean operator, median operator, or kernel based mode operator are adopted (Kourentzes, 2014). With the proliferation of the ensemble concept, many applications of ANN ensembles for forecasting have been developed and tested. Examples can be found in the areas of economic modeling (Bai & Ng, 2008; Ha, Cho, & MacLachlan, 2005; Inoue & Kilian, 2008; Stock & Watson 2006;), financial and commodities trading (Bodyanskiy & Popov, 2006; Chen & Leung, 2004; Kourentzes, Barrow, & Crone, 2014), and supply chain management (Kleijnen 2005; Trapero, Kourentzes, & Fildes, 2012).

Selection of Bootstrap Sample Size

In recent years, bootstrap methods have become a common tool in empirical research. When usual approximations are unattainable or other methods are invalid, bootstrap is able to provide more accurate answers (Wehrens, Putter, & Buydens, 2000). After Efron (1979) introduced the bootstrap method, a large number of papers were published developing new bootstrap schemes (e.g., Davison & Hinkley, 1997; Mammen, 2012; Rubin, 1981; Wu, 1986), and building mathematical foundations (especially the asymptotic properties) (Bickel, 1981; Efron, 1992a; Mammen, 2012; Shao, 2012). Generally speaking, bootstrap has been used primarily for but not limited to estimating standard error estimate, generating confidence interval, and testing hypothesis. Although it is easy to implement a bootstrap method with the power of a modern computer, determining an optimal (or at least a good) number of bootstrap samples used in resampling is still in a somewhat ad-hoc manner (Andrews & Buchinsky, 2002).

Efron and Tibshirani (1986) utilized the coefficient of variation of the bootstrap standard error estimator to estimate the true standard error. Based on the formula for this estimation, Efron suggested a range of values of bootstrap sample size. Because this formula contains some unknown parameters, this range may not be accurate (Andrews & Buchinsky, 2002).

Andrews and Buchinsky (2000) developed a three-step method for choosing the number of bootstrap samples. Later, Andrews and Buchinsky (2002) systematically discussed the issues of bootstrap sample size in relation to bootstrap standard errors, confidence intervals, and hypothesis testing. Their proposed method is versatile and applicable to parametric, semiparametric, and nonparametric models with either independent or dependent data. The method also works well on moving blocked bootstraps for time series data.

Many studies suggested using the bootstrap method with a sample size of 100 to 500 (Wehrens, Putter, & Buydens, 2000). Considering the increasing power of modern computation, he also suggested that we may not be confined by this number. In practice, the error of Monte Carlo bootstrap approximation to a statistic has two error sources. The first one is the bootstrap error, which is inevitable and independent of bootstrap sample size. The second one is Monte Carlo error. In order to properly select the bootstrap sample size, it is reasonable to choose the one in such a way as to reduce Monte Carlo error. Jackknife-after-bootstrap is a method to evaluate the bootstrap error and Monte Carlo error (Efron 1992b). Davison and Hinkley (1997) recommended taking $B \approx 40n$ where B is the number of bootstrap samples, and n is the sample size of the original data.

METHODOLOGIES

In this section, we briefly summarize the two types of neural network models: *multilayer feed forward neural network* and *general regression neural network*, used in this study. Also, we discuss how bootstrap aggregation (also called bagging) can be used to improve the performance of the neural network models.

Multilayer Feed Forward Neural Network (MLFN)

Multilayer feed forward neural network is a well-established neural network model, which is usually coupled with the back propagation training algorithm. It has been applied to solve numerous practical problems in business forecasting and engineering management (e.g., Tkac & Verner, 2016).

Typically, a MLFN consists of several layers of neurons. The first layer is called the input layer, and the last layer is called an output layer. All other layers in between are hidden layers, which are so called because they do not directly interface with external input/output connectors. There is no specific restriction on the number of hidden layers a MLFN should have. However, under normal circumstances, it is not recommended to have more than two hidden layers. An essential feature of MLFN is that information flow within the structure of the network has to be feed-forward, which implies that no feedback loops exist. In general, the neurons on one layer are fully connected to all neurons in successive layers. This architectural design ensures that the outputs are the results of explicit functions of inputs and corresponding weights.

A typical (basic form of) MLFN is shown in Figure 1.1. This architectural design shows a MLFN with five inputs, one hidden layer with three neurons, and a single output in the output layer. Mathematically, the output of neuron in the hidden layer is the weighted linear combination of inputs:

$$a_j = \sum_{i=1}^{d} w_{ji}^{(k)} x_i \qquad (1.1)$$

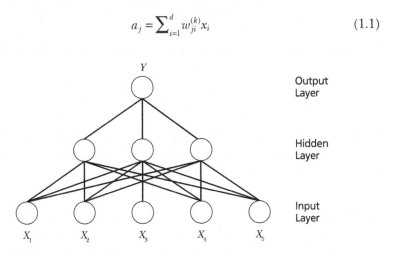

Figure 1.1 Typical MLFN architectural design.

where $w_{ji}^{(k)}$ is the weight from input neuron i to hidden neuron j. Then an activation function is applied on a_j, to transform the linear combination, as shown in Equation (1.1) to its output. Two widely adopted activation functions are the logistic sigmoid activation function (Equation 1.2) and $\tanh(x)$ activation function (Equation 1.3).

$$g(x) = \frac{1}{1+\exp(-x)} \qquad (1.2)$$

$$g(x) = \tanh(x) = \frac{e^x - e^{-x}}{e^x + e^{-x}} \qquad (1.3)$$

To train the network, the weights are changed according to the error from the output when compared to the expected value. This process is carried out through a generalized least mean square method, called back propagation. First, the parameters of the network are fixed, then the error of input passing through each layer is calculated by Equation 1.4:

$$e_j(n) = d_j(n) - y_j(n) \qquad (1.4)$$

where $e_j(n)$ denotes the error of jth neuron from input n, $d_j(n)$ is the expected value, and $y_j(n)$ is the actual output from the network.

Subsequently, the error $e_j(n)$ is propagated through the network backwards. In this process, the free parameters are adjusted in response to reduce the error given in Equation 1.5:

$$\varepsilon(n) = \tfrac{1}{2} \sum_j \left(d_j(n) - y_j(n) \right)^2 \qquad (1.5)$$

By gradient descent algorithm, the change in weight is shown in Equation 1.6:

$$\Delta \omega_{ji}(n) = -\eta \frac{\partial \varepsilon(n)}{\partial v_j(n)} y_i(n) \qquad (1.6)$$

where η is the learning rate which needs to be selected to assure that the weights are able to converge rapidly, y_i is the output of previous neuron, and the derivative to be calculated depends on the current neuron.

General Regression Neural Network (GRNN)

GRNN, first proposed and developed by Specht (1991), is another design of neural network with supervised training. Unlike MLFN, GRNN is based on the statistical foundation of nonparametric regression. This means that the network requires a sequential presentation and memorization of training samples for the state space rather than an iterative optimization process as used in the back propagation algorithm for the training of MLFN. Therefore, the advantages of GRNN lie in the ability to achieve the convergence of weights with only a few samples. Also, with the increasing of sample size, the error converges to zero. As implied by its name, GRNN can be, theoretically, used to approximate any target function, thanks to the notion of a statistical learning technique called kernel regression. The underlying mathematical concept of estimation using GRNN is summarized in Equation 1.7:

$$E\left[y\middle|X\right] = \frac{\int_{-\infty}^{\infty} yf(X,y)\,dy}{\int_{-\infty}^{\infty} f(X,y)\,dy} \tag{1.7}$$

where y is the predicted output from GRNN, X is the input vector. $E\left[y\middle|X\right]$ is the expectation of output y given an input vector X, and $f(X, y)$ is the joint probability density function.

The architectural design of GRNN is also different from that of MLFN. GRNN has a more stringent design and consists of exactly four layers of neurons: input layer, pattern layer, summation layer, and output layer. A typical GRNN architectural design with four input attributes is depicted in Figure 1.2. The input layer, which is connected to the pattern layer, is used for receiving information. The pattern layer then combines and processes

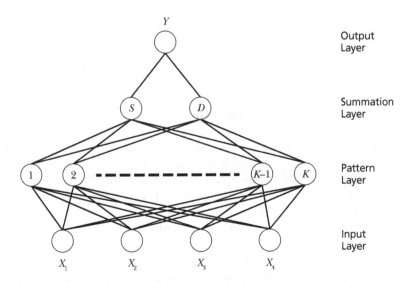

Figure 1.2 Typical GRNN architectural design.

information. The number of neurons in this layer is the same as the number of cases (K) in the training sample. There is a transfer function associated with each pattern neuron, which is analogous to the activation function found in a hidden neuron in MLFN. In the original design by Specht (1991), the transfer function takes on the multivariate Gaussian distribution form:

$$\theta_i = e^{-(X-U_i)'(X-U_i)/2\sigma^2} \tag{1.8}$$

where U_i is the training vector of neuron i in the pattern layer, X is the input vector, and s is the smoothing (control) parameter.

The pattern layer then passes the outputs from activation function to the summation layer, which is composed of two types of neurons. The D summation neuron calculated the unweighted sum of outputs from pattern layer, as given by Equation 1.9. On the other hand, S summation neuron transform the inputs from the pattern layer into a weighted output, as shown in Equation 1.10. The neurons in the output layer divide the output of the S summation neuron by that of the D summation neuron in order to obtain the estimate y as in Equation 1.11. For the multivariate version, the final GRNN regression output is $Y = [y_1, y_2, \ldots y_M]$ where there are M elements in the output vector Y.

$$S_D = \Sigma_i \, \theta_i \tag{1.9}$$

$$S_S = \Sigma_i \, w_i \theta_i \tag{1.10}$$

$$y = \frac{S_S}{S_D} = \frac{\Sigma_i \, w_i \theta_i}{\Sigma_i \, \theta_i} \tag{1.11}$$

Bootstrap Aggregation (Bagging)

Bootstrap aggregation (aka, bagging) is one of the widely used algorithmic framework to enhance machine learning. From a statistical perspective, it is an averaging method applied to estimation through the creation of a set of bootstrap samples. The primary goal of bagging is to improve the stability and accuracy of prediction by reducing variance and lightening the likelihood of over-fitting, a common yet detrimental side effect from the training of neural network.

Suppose a sample data set **D** contains n observations. Through uniformly re-sampling from **D** with replacement, bagging creates new bootstrap sample data sets D^{*b}, for $b = 1, 2, \ldots, B$ and B is the total number of bootstrap samples created. In other words, the process of resampling is re-iterated with the original set **D** for a total of B times. During each iteration in bootstrapping, n^* observations are created. It should be noted that there is no absolute requirement that n^* has to be identical to n.

After the creation of B bootstrap samples, each of these samples is used one by one for in-sample training with respect to an estimation model (such as a neural network). Simply put, the model is fitted on each bootstrap sample to get the prediction $\hat{f}^{*b}(x)$ based on bootstrap sample b. With a total number of B bootstrap samples, a total of B predicted values of $\hat{f}^{*b}(x)$ are generated. Finally, the B predicted values are "aggregated" to form the estimate from bagging. Equation 1.12 shows the un-weighted aggregation from B bootstrap estimations:

$$\hat{f}_{\text{bag}}(x) = \frac{1}{B}\sum_{b=1}^{B}\hat{f}^{*b}(x) \qquad (1.12)$$

Interested readers can refer to Breiman (1996) and Maimon and Rokach (2005) for a technical exposition of the method.

DATA AND EMPIRICAL EXPERIMENT

Supply Chain Order Data and Preprocessing

The dataset utilized in the empirical experiment is furnished by a component manufacturer located in Hong Kong. The manufacturer specializes in the production and electroplating of metallic alloy components used in a variety of consumer products (such as toys and electronic devices.) This manufacturer represents the upstream partner, whereas its customer is the downstream vendor partner in the two-stage supply chain described previously in the beginning of this chapter. Because of the subcontracting nature in their supply chain relationship, the order quantities placed by the vendor fluctuate periodically and often are not known well in advance.

In the current study, we specifically examine a product family consisting of three items of identical design but of different colors: gray, gold, and silver. The gray item does not require any electroplating while the gold and silver ones have to be processed with respective electroplating. From both operational and accounting control perspectives, the three items can and should be combined and treated as a single entity. Thus, our empirical experiment focuses on the consolidated order quantity and forecast of the entire product family rather than individual items.

The entire dataset covers 97 monthly periods running from July 2007 through July 2015. To serve the blind evaluation purpose, the data set is divided into two subsets: the in-sample training set (72 months from July 2007 through June 2013) and the out-of-sample testing set (25 months from July 2013 through July 2015). This breakdown scheme utilizes approximately 74% of all data for model training and selection and about 26% for holdout testing of different forecasting models.

Further, several transformations are applied to the original supply chain order data. First, each data series of an item is normalized according to Equation 1.13. This measure is taken in order to eliminate the potential of an incomparable data dimensional scaling issue or spurious fitting due to inconsistent variances occurring within the orders of the three items. They are of the same design, but their order quantities fluctuate in dissimilar manners.

$$x'_{ik} = \frac{x_{ik} - \mu_k}{\sigma_k} \tag{1.13}$$

where x'_{ik} is the normalized order quantity of item k (for $k = 1, 2, 3$) in period i, μ_k and σ_k are the mean and standard deviation of item k's order quantity over the entire experimental horizon. Then, the normalized order quantities of the three items are aggregated into a consolidated order quantity for the product family, as shown in Equation 1.14.

$$x'_i = \sum_{k=1}^{3} x'_{ik} \tag{1.14}$$

Finally, the consolidated order quantity for the product family is rescaled to the range from –1 to +1, inclusively. This is necessary for the training and operation of MLFN with sigmoidal activation function although it is not required for GRNN and ARIMA. However, for a fair comparison among forecasting models, the same rescaled data series is used in the analyses by all models. The rescaling is performed as follow:

$$x' = \frac{x'_i - x'_{min}}{x'_{max} - x'_{min}} \tag{1.15}$$

where x' is the rescaled order quantity for the product family and x'_{min} and x'_{max} are the minimum and maximum observations, respectively, within the consolidated order quantity data series.

Training and Selection of Neural Network Specification

As described in "Methodologies," training of a neural network is inherently regulated by its own set of control parameters (or hyperparameters) and the underlying model specification. Thus, selection of the parameters and specification will directly influence the quality of order forecast, not to mention the inventory level as well as the profitability of the supply chain partners. In order to obtain a fair and more robust comparative evaluation of MLFN and GRNN's performances, each type of neural network architecture is trained by different sets of control parameters and different model specifications. In the case of MLFN, network architectures based on different combinations of the number of hidden neurons and the number of hidden layers are examined. In addition, different lagged variables in the input vector are investigated. On the other hand, because of GRNN's more rigid architectural design, only different lag terms in the input vector are applied to the training of GRNN. In this fashion, an array of MLFN and GRNN models, all with different control parameters and/or model specifications, are trained and in-sample performance statistics (such as MSE and MPE) are computed for these trained networks. The best model in terms of the quality of forecast (i.e., performance statistics) is then selected from each domain of MLFN and GRNN models. For the sake of brevity, performance statistics covering the in-sample training period of this diverse array of neural networks are not reported here. Subsequently, these two best models are used for out-of-sample comparative evaluation and bagging enhancement (to be explained in the next section).

Bootstrap Aggregation for Neural Network (Bagging)

For bootstrap aggregation, we follow the proposed bagging framework outlined in "Bootstrap Aggregation (Bagging)" (which, in turn, is derived from Maimon & Rokach, 2005). Specifically, a total of $B = 10$ bootstrap samples are generated. Then, each of these 10 samples is fed to the best MLFN model selected by their in-sample performance. In other words, the MLFN is trained 10 separate times, each time by a particular set of $b = 1, 2, \ldots, B$ bootstrap sample data. Detailed procedures of the training and selection of neural networks have been documented in the previous section. The trained network is then used to forecast the order quantities over the out-of-sample evaluation subperiod. As a consequence, 10 series of 25 out-of-sample forecasts are estimated with each series corresponding to a particular bootstrap sample. Finally, the 10 order forecasts for a certain monthly period are averaged out to become the "aggregated" forecast from the MLFN-bagging framework. This entire bagging paradigm is repeated for GRNN.

It should be noted that the number of bootstrap samples (B) will be increased to 20 and 30 in the auxiliary experiment. This change allows us to examine the impact of the number of bootstrap samples, which can be viewed as a proxy of computational burden, on the improvement of neural network forecast quality.

RESULTS AND DISCUSSION

As described in the previous section, an array of neural networks based upon MLFN and GRNN architectures with different control parameters and model specifications are created in our experiment. Their performances over the in-sample (training) subperiod are then measured and the best models, one from MLFN and one from GRNN, in terms of forecast quality are selected for out-of-sample blind evaluation. In addition, these two models serve as the "basis" neural networks used in our proposed bootstrap aggregation framework (refer to "Methodologies" and "Data and Empirical Experiment" for details of bagging.) Subsequently, out-of-sample performances of MLFN and GRNN used in conjunction with the bagging framework are measured accordingly.

Table 1.1 reports various performance statistics for supply chain order forecasting over the out-of-sample (holdout) subperiod from July 2013 through July 2015. The results indicate the quality of forecasts for MLFN and GRNN for two scenarios: when the bagging enhancement is and is not utilized. In order to conduct a more comprehensive evaluation of the learning networks, the results are benchmarked against the more conventional linear method of ARIMA and the random walk model (i.e., the null case of no forecast). Five performance measures based on four statistical tests are tabulated in the table: R^2, mean percentage error (MPE), U statistic, and the regressed bias (α) and proportion coefficients (β) from Theil's Decomposition Test (Theil 1966).

Loosely speaking, U statistic is the ratio of the RMSE of a model's forecasts to the RMSE of the random walk forecasts of no change in the consolidated (i.e., product family's) order quantity. Since the random walk

TABLE 1.1 Performance Statistics for Out-of-Sample Supply Chain Order Forecasting

	R^2	MPE	U Statistic	Bias Coefficient (α)	Proportion Coefficient (β)
ARIMA	0.6268	33.61%	0.4274	0.2864	0.7934
MLFN without bagging	0.8154	16.66%	0.2119	0.1639	0.8812
MLFN with bagging	0.8926	11.46%	0.1457	0.1281	0.9207
GRNN without bagging	0.8618	14.91%	0.1896	0.1537	0.8678
GRNN with bagging	0.8930	10.87%	0.1393	0.1295	0.9311
Random walk	0.2605	78.64%		0.6043	0.4645

Note: 10 bootstrap samples (*B*) are used when the bagging framework is applied to neural network forecasting. No bootstrap re-sampling is used for models of ARIMA, random walk, and neural networks without bagging.

forecast of next month's order quantity is equal to the current month's observed order quantity, a U statistic of less than 1 implies that the tested model outperforms the random walk model during the out-of-sample period. On the contrary, a U statistic exceeding 1 implies that the forecasting capability of the tested model is not meaningful as it cannot outperform the case of no forecasting. It should be noted that U statistic is a unit-free measurement and can be directly compared across different models. Makridakis, Wheelwright and McGee (1983) provide a more detailed exposition of this statistical analysis.

Theil's Decomposition Test (Theil, 1966) is carried out by a linear regression of the actual observed consolidated order quantity (x_i') on the tested model's consolidated order quantity forecast $(\widehat{x_i'})$ and a constant:

$$x_i' = \beta \widehat{x_i'} + \alpha \tag{1.16}$$

If the tested model yields high quality forecast persistently, the constant α (bias coefficient) should be indifferent to zero and the estimated coefficient β (proportion coefficient) should be indifferent to one. Interested readers can refer to Leung, Chen, and Daouk (2000) for an extra example of this test applied to another business context.

From Table 1.1, it is apparent that both learning networks substantially outperform the more conventional ARIMA forecasting and random walk models in all five performance measures. In other words, MLFN and GRNN based neural network forecasting, which rests on nonlinear, nonparametric statistical learning, provides more accurate order quantity predictions than ARIMA forecasting, which is abided by linearity and parametric assumptions. Needless to elaborate, all forecasting models are better than the scenario of not having an educated forecast. This conclusion is best illustrated by the small magnitudes of the computed U statistics for all forecasting models. Besides, the smaller estimated bias coefficients (α) from neural network models suggest that the learning machines leads to a lesser degree of bias relative to ARIMA.

Likewise, network models' larger proportion coefficients (β) are much closer to one than ARIMA, implying a better alignment of forecasts and the actual movement of supply chain order quantity.

Furthermore, it can be seen that MLFN with bagging and GRNN with bagging outperform their no-bagging counterparts. This is substantiated by a gain in R^2 along with material reductions in MPE and U statistics when bagging is applied to the two neural network models. Consequently, the net changes due to bagging enhancement are computed and displayed in Table 1.2. The results reveal that not only do MLFN and GRNN benefit from bagging, they also improve in varying degrees. In this case, MLFN's gain in R^2 and reduction in MPE and U statistics are higher than those of GRNN. When this finding is

TABLE 1.2 Net Change in Out-of-Sample Neural Network Forecasting Performance When Bootstrap Aggregation Framework (Bagging Enhancement) Is Utilized

	MLFN	GRNN
Net Gain in R^2	0.0772	0.0312
% Gain in R^2	9.47%	3.62%
Net Reduction in MPE	5.20	4.04
% Reduction in MPE	31.21%	27.10%
Net Reduction in U	0.0662	0.0503
% Reduction in U	31.24%	26.53%

compared with the results in Table 1.1, it is postulated that GRNN has already been doing better than MLFN without the use of bagging and, thereby, the improvement from bagging enhancement is less prominent. This may suggest that the benefit from bagging may be capped to a certain maximum limit, depending on the data structure and neural network design. However, further experimentation is required to confirm these notions.

Bootstrap aggregation is a resampling framework and thus is subject to implementation issues regarding the selections of the number of bootstrap samples (B) and the size of each bootstrap sample (n^*). Given the success of the bagging enhancement, it is imperative to explore these issues and the degree of effect on the performance of a neural network. To create a sharper focus in the current study and allow a parallel comparison with models without bagging, we fix the size of each bootstrap sample to 72, the number of monthly observations in the original in-sample (training) subperiod. In short, this means $n^* = n$. Hence, the size of the training sample for all tested models remains constant. As a consequence, the empirical exploration can shed light directly on the impact of the number of bootstrap samples on a learning network's forecasting performance (without the worry of potential interaction effect.)

In light of this, an auxiliary experiment is devised to measure the impact of bagging with an increasing number of bootstrap samples. It should be noted that the base case, as reported in Tables 1.1 and 1.2, embraces 10 bootstrap samples (i.e., $B = 10$) during the bagging enhancement process. The number of samples is raised to $B = 20$ and 30, respectively, in the auxiliary experiment. Performance measures of R^2, MPE, and U statistic for varying level of bootstrapping are computed and shown in Table 1.3. It can be observed that the three performance criteria improve when the number of the bootstrap sample increases. However, this increasing trend comes at a decreasing rate; that is, the marginal improvement from $B = 0$ to 10, to 20 to 30 samples deteriorates. Simply put, the benefit of adopting more bootstrap samples fades away. This is possibly because the aggregation of

TABLE 1.3   Effect of the Number of Bootstrap Samples on Out-of-Sample Neural Network Forecasting Performance With Respect to Different Neural Network Architectures

	R^2	MPE	U Statistic
MLFN without bagging (B = 0)	0.8154	16.66%	0.2119
MLFN with bagging			
B = 10 bootstrap samples	0.8926	11.46%	0.1457
B = 20 bootstrap samples	0.9103	11.21%	0.1416
B = 30 bootstrap samples	0.9150	10.97%	0.1396
GRNN without bagging (B = 0)	0.8618	14.91%	0.1896
GRNN with bagging			
B = 10 bootstrap samples	0.8930	10.87%	0.1393
B = 20 bootstrap samples	0.8982	10.52%	0.1329
B = 30 bootstrap samples	0.9104	10.06%	0.1267

bootstrap samples leads to a general long-term reduction of variance in forecasts, resulting in more reliable order forecasts and hopefully smaller error in order quantity. When a reasonably large number of bootstrap samples is used in the bagging framework, most of the variance reduction is realized through aggregation. Therefore, using even more samples will not create proportionally more impact.

This notion is depicted by the plots of the number of bootstrap samples versus R^2, MPE, and U statistic in Figures 1.3, 1.4, and 1.5, respectively. In each figure, the forecast performance improves but slows down and levels off in a plateau. This pattern suggests that a diminishing marginal return in terms of performance when more computation, which is proportional to the number of bootstrap samples, is utilized in the order forecasting

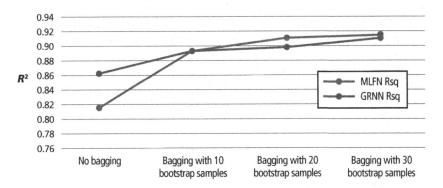

Figure 1.3   Effect of the number of bootstrap samples on out-of-sample R^2 with respect to different neural network architectures.

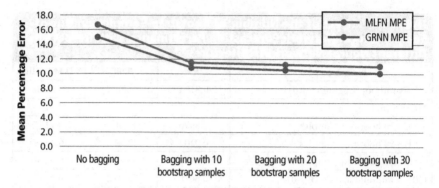

Figure 1.4   Effect of the number of bootstrap samples on out-of-sample MPE with respect to different neural network architectures.

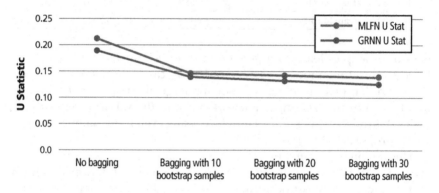

Figure 1. 5   Effect of the number of bootstrap samples on out-of-sample U statistic with respect to different neural network architectures.

process. It also implies that the number of bootstrap samples and, thereby, computation used can be capped (after a certain level) without a major sacrifice in order forecast accuracy. This finding is especially meaningful when computing resource or allocated computational time is extremely constrained. Further, the same conclusions can be drawn for both MLFN and GRNN, although improvement via bagging may occur at varying rates when different network designs are adopted.

CONCLUSIONS

In this study, we demonstrate how to apply the bootstrap aggregation (also commonly known as bagging) framework to neural network forecasting and, at the same time, to resolve some imperative issues (such as consolidation of product family items and data preprocessing) related to the prediction of order quantity in supply chain planning. In addition, we explore how the number of bootstrap samples, which reflects the required level of computational burden, affects the performance of the neural network forecasts.

Specifically, the original product data are preprocessed and divided into two subsamples for in-sample training and out-of-sample testing. MLFN and GRNN with different combinations of control parameter settings and model specifications are trained with the in-sample data. Their in-sample performances are measured and the best model in terms of forecast quality is selected: one for MLFN and one for GRNN. When our bagging framework is applied to the ANN forecasting, bootstrap samples are generated from the preprocessed supply chain order data set according to the standard bagging procedure. Each of these bootstrap samples are then used for the in-sample training of different ANNs, yielding a diverse set of out-of-sample estimated paths of changes in downstream orders. This entire empirical process is repeated with different numbers of bootstrap samples.

Results are benchmarked with order quantity forecasts from corresponding ANNs of no bagging, conventional ARIMA, and random walk models. Our finding indicates that the bagging framework enhances the overall performance and creates more persistent accuracy in order forecasts over the longer run. Moreover, improvement in performance due to bagging is significant but varies across different neural network designs. It was also found that the performance of forecasting with bagging follows the pattern of diminishing marginal return. In other words, performance improves at a decreasing rate with an increasing level of computation (the number of bootstraps). These conclusions hold for different network architectural designs, although the impact of bagging enhancement is not uniform with different neural networks.

Future extension of the current work should include an examination of how the supply chain's order lumpiness affects the forecast quality of the bagging framework, as well as the choice of the number of bootstrap samples. Future research can also address the problem from the perspective of aggregate production planning (APP) where rough estimates of aggregate product family production volumes are needed for intermediate term planning purposes. It will be useful to know whether or not forecasting the product family as a whole is better than the procedure of forecasting individual product items separately and then aggregating the forecasts into one for the family.

NOTE

1. Corresponding author. Department of Management Science and Statistics, College of Business, University of Texas, San Antonio, TX 78249. Tel: 210-458-5776. Fax: 210-458-6350. Email: mtleung@utsa.edu

REFERENCES

Andrews, D. W., & Buchinsky, M. (2000). A three-step method for choosing the number of bootstrap repetitions. *Econometrica, 68*, 23–51.

Andrews, D. W., & Buchinsky, M. (2002). On the number of bootstrap repetitions for BCa confidence intervals. *Econometric Theory, 18*, 962–984.

Bai, J., & Ng, S. (2008). Forecasting economic time series using targeted predictors. *Journal of Econometrics, 146*, 304–317.

Bickel, P. J., & Freedman, D. A. (1981). Some asymptotic theory for the bootstrap. *The Annals of Statistics, 9*, 1196–1217.

Bodyanskiy, Y., & Popov, S. (2006). Neural network approach to forecasting of quasiperiodic financial time series. *European Journal of Operational Research, 175*, 1357–1366.

Breiman, L. (1996). Bagging predictors. *Machine Learning, 24*, 123–140.

Breiman L. (1999). Prediction games and arcing algorithms. *Neural Computation, 11*, 1493–517.

Büchlmann, P., & Yu, B. (2002). Analyzing bagging. *Annals of Statistics, 30*(6), 927–961.

Buja, A., & Stuetzle, W. (2000). The effect of bagging on variance, bias, and mean squared error. *Preprint. AT&T Labs-Research.* Retrieved from http://www.research.att.com/~andreas/\#nonpar}

Carbonneau, R., Laframboise, K., & Vahidov, R. (2008). Application of machine learning techniques for supply chain demand forecasting. *European Journal of Operational Research, 184*, 1140.

Chandra, A., & Yao, X. (2006). Evolving hybrid ensembles of learning machines for better generalisation. *Neurocomputing, 69*, 686–700.

Chase, C. W. (2013). *Demand-driven forecasting: A structured approach to forecasting.* Hoboken, NJ: John Wiley.

Chen, A. S., & Leung, M. T. (2004). Regression neural network for error correction in foreign exchange forecasting and trading. *Computers & Operations Research, 31*(7), 1049–1068.

Chen, R., & Yu, J. (2007). An improved bagging neural network ensemble algorithm and its application. *Third International Conference on Natural* Computation, *5*, 730–734.

Chopra, S., & Meindl,P. (2016). *Supply chain management: Strategy, planning, and operation* (6th ed.). Upper Saddle River, NJ: Pearson.

Claveria, O., Monte, E., & Torra, S. (2015). Tourism demand forecasting with neural network models: Different ways of treating information. *International Journal of Tourism Research, 17*, 492–500.

Clémençon, S., & Vayatis, N. (2009). Tree-based ranking methods. *IEEE Transactions on Information Theory, 55*, 4316–4336.

Clyde, M., & Lee, H. (2001). Bagging and the Bayesian bootstrap. In *Artificial intelligence and statistics.* Burlington MA: Morgan Kaufmann.

Croston, J. D. (1972). Forecasting and stock control for intermittent demands. *Operational Research Quarterly, 23*, 289–304.

Davison, A. C., & Hinkley, D. V. (1997). *Bootstrap methods and their applications.* Cambridge, England: Cambridge University Press.

Dietterich, T. G. (2000). Ensemble methods in machine learning. In *International Workshop on Multiple Classifier Systems* (pp. 1–15). Berlin, Germany: Springer Berlin Heidelberg.

Efron, B. (1979). Bootstrap methods: Another look at the jackknife. *Annals of Statistics, 7,* 126.

Efron, B. (1992a). Bootstrap methods: Another look at the jackknife. In S. Kotz, & N. L. Johnson *Breakthroughs in statistics* (Vol. 3; pp. 569–593). New York, NY: Springer-Verlag.

Efron, B. (1992b). Jackknife-after-bootstrap standard errors and influence functions. *Journal of the Royal Statistical Society, Series B (Methodological),* 83–127.

Efron, B., & Tibshirani, R. (1986). Bootstrap methods for standard errors, confidence intervals, and other measures of statistical accuracy. *Statistical Science, 1*(1), 1–35.

Friedman, J. H., & Hall, P. (2007). On bagging and nonlinear estimation. *Journal of Statistical Planning and Inference, 137,* 669–683.

Gutierreza, R. S., Solis, A. O, & Mukhopadhyay, S. (2008). Lumpy demand forecasting using neural networks. *International Journal of Production Economics, 111,* 409–420.

Ha, K., Cho, S., & MacLachlan, D. (2005). Response models based on bagging neural networks. *Journal of Interactive Marketing, 19*(1), 17–30.

Heravi, S., Osborn, D. R., & Birchenhall, C.R. (2004). Linear versus neural network forecasts for European industrial production series. *International Journal of Forecasting, 20,* 435–446.

Hill, T., O'Connor, M., & Remus, W., (1996). Neural network models for time series forecasts. *Management Science, 42,* 1082–1092.

Hornik, K., Stinchcombe, M., & White, H. (1989). Multilayer feedforward networks are universal approximators. *Neural Networks, 2,* 359–366.

Iman, R. L., & Conover, W. J. (1988). *Modern business statistics.* New York, NY: John Wiley.

Inoue, A., & Kilian, L. (2008). How useful is bagging in forecasting economic time series? A case study of U.S. consumer price inflation. *Journal of the American Statistical Association, 103*(482), 511–522.

Khwaja, A. S., Naeem, M., Anpalagan, A., Venetsanopoulos, A., & Venkatesh, B. (2015). Improved short-term load forecasting using bagged neural networks. *Electric Power Systems Research, 125,* 109–115.

Kleijnen, J. P. (2005). Supply chain simulation tools and techniques: A survey. *International Journal of Simulation and Process Modelling, 1*(1/2), 82–89.

Kourentzes, N. (2013). Intermittent demand forecasts with neural networks. *International Journal of Production Economics, 143,* 198–206.

Kourentzes, N., Barrow, D. K., & Crone, S. F. (2014). Neural network ensemble operators for time series forecasting. *Expert Systems with Applications, 41*(9), 4235–4244.

Krogh, A., & Vedelsby, J. (1995). Neural network ensembles, cross validation, and active learning. *Advances in Neural Information Processing Systems, 7,* 231–238.

Lau, H. C. W., Ho, G. T. S., & Zhao, Y. (2013). A demand forecast model using a combination of surrogate data analysis and optimal neural network approach. *Decision Support Systems, 54,* 1404

Leung, M. T., Chen, A. S, & Daouk, H. (2000). Forecasting exchange rates using general regression neural network. *Computers and Operations Research, 27,* 1093–1110.

Leung, M. T., Chen, A. S., & Mancha, R. (2009). Making trading decisions for financial engineered derivatives: A novel ensemble of neural networks using information content. *Intelligent Systems in Accounting, Finance and Management, 16,* 257–277.

Leung, M. T., Quintana, R., & Chen, A. S. (2009). Make-to-order product demand forecasting: exponential smoothing models with neural network correction. In K. Lawrence & R. K. Klimberg, *Advances in business and management forecasting* (Vol. 6). Bingley, England: Emerald.

Mabert, V. A., (1978). Forecast modification based upon residual analysis: A case study of check volume estimation. *Decision Sciences, 9,* 285–296.

Maimon, O., & Rokach, L. (2005). *Decomposition methodology for knowledge discovery and data mining.* Singapore: World Scientific.

Makridakis, S., Andersen, A., Carbone, R., Fildes, R., Hibon, M., Lewandowski, R., Newton, J., Parzen, E., & Winkler, R. (1982). The accuracy of extrapolation (time series) methods: Results of a forecasting competition. *Journal of Forecasting 1,* 111–153.

Makridakis, S. G., Wheelwright, S. C., & Hyndman, R. J. (1998). *Forecasting: Methods and applications.* (3rd ed.). New York, NY: John Wiley.

Makridakis, S, G., Wheelwright, S. C., & McGee, V. E. (1983). *Forecasting: Methods and applications* (2nd ed.). New York, NY: John Wiley.

Mammen, E. (2012). *When does bootstrap work? Asymptotic results and simulations* (Vol. 77): *Lecture notes in statistics series.* Berlin, Germany: Springer-Verlag.

Pour, A. N., Tabar, B. R., & Rahimzadeh, A., (2008). A hybrid neural network and traditional approach for forecasting lumpy demand. *Proceedings of World Academy of Science: Engineering & Technology, 42,* 384–390.

Quintana, R., & Leung, M. T. (2007). Adaptive exponential smoothing versus conventional approaches for lumpy demand forecasting: case of production planning for a manufacturing line. *International Journal of Production Research, 45,* 4937–4957.

Rubin, D. B. (1981). The Bayesian bootstrap. *The Annals of Statistics, 9,* 130–134.

Shao, J., & Tu, D. (2012). *The jackknife and bootstrap.* Dordrecht, the Netherlands: Springer.

Specht, D. (1991). A general regression neural network. *IEEE Transactions on Neural Networks, 2,* 568–576.

Stock, J. H., & Watson, M. W. (2006). Forecasting with many predictors. *Handbook of Economic Forecasting, 1,* 515–554.

Syntetos, A. A., & Boylan, J. E. (2005). The accuracy of intermittent demand estimates. *International Journal of Forecasting, 21,* 303–314.

Syntetos, A. A., Nikolopoulos, K., & Boylan, J. E. (2010). Judging the judges through accuracy implication metrics: The case of inventory forecasting. *International Journal of Forecasting, 26,* 134–143.

Teunter, R., & Sani, B. (2009). Calculating order-up-to levels for products with intermittent demand. *International Journal of Production Economics, 118,* 82–86.

Theil, H. (1966). *Applied economic forecasting.* Amsterdam, the Netherlands: North Holland.

Thomassey, S. (2010). Sales forecasts in clothing industry: The key success factor of the supply chain management. *International Journal of Production Economics, 128,* 470.

Tkac, M., & Verner, R. (2016). Artificial neural networks in business: Two decades of research. *Applied Soft Computing, 38,* 788–804.

Trapero, J. R., Kourentzes, N., & Fildes, R. (2012). Impact of information exchange on supplier forecasting performance. *Omega, 40*(6), 738–747.

Tsai, J. M, & Hung, S. W. (2016). Supply chain relationship quality and performance in technological turbulence: An artificial neural network approach. *International Journal of Production Research, 54,* 2757–2770.

Venkatesh, K., Ravi, V., Prinzie, A., & Van den Poel, D. (2014). Cash demand forecasting in ATMs by clustering and neural networks. *European Journal of Operational Research, 232,* 383–392.

Weese, M., Martinze, W., Megahed, F. M., & Jones-Farmer, L. A. (2016). Statistical learning models applied to process monitoring: An overview and perspective. *Journal of Quality Technology, 48,* 4–27.

Wehrens, R., Putter, H., & Buydens, L. M. (2000). The bootstrap: A tutorial. *Chemometrics and Intelligent Laboratory Systems, 54,* 35–52.

West, D., Dellana, S., & Qian, J. (2005). Neural network ensemble strategies for financial decision applications. *Computers and Operations Research, 32,* 2543–2559.

White, H., (1992). *Artificial neural networks: Approximation and learning theory.* Oxford, England: Blackwell.

Wu, C. F. J. (1986). Jackknife, bootstrap and other resampling methods in regression analysis. *The Annals of Statistics, 14*(4), 1261–1295.

Zhou, Z. H., Wu, J., & Tang, W. (2002). Ensembling neural networks: Many could be better than all. *Artificial Intelligence, 137,* 239–263.

CHAPTER 2

COMBINING RETROSPECTIVE AND PREDICTIVE ANALYTICS FOR MORE ROBUST DECISION SUPPORT

Thomas Ott
Rapid Miner

Stephan Kudyba
New Jersey Institute of Technology

ABSTRACT

Business Intelligence (BI) systems and software have seen explosive growth and adoption over the past decade, where Key Performance Indicator (KPI) dashboards have become common place in organizations across industries. This aggressive adoption of reporting and visual based analytics has increased the curiosity of decision makers to go beyond information that presents retrospective views and delves into information that answers "why" things are happening and "what's likely to happen." Advanced methods such as machine learning and regression and data mining applications provide this information. The dream was to "marry" these two systems together and allow for a truly comprehensive picture of a company's health. This chapter illustrates a complementary link between a retrospective dashboard platform and data mining capabilities to facilitate decision support that addresses not only "what has" and "what is happening" with customer churn but also "what is likely" to happen. This is accomplished with an e-based visualization api.

The utilization of business intelligence (BI) systems has experienced noteworthy growth over the past decade as the evolution of the digital economy continues to progress. However, as innovations in information technology and data resources have increased in sophistication and depth, so to have the functional requirements of decision support platforms to meet end-user demands. BI has largely involved a retrospective focus regarding organizational performance, where advanced/predictive analytics often remain an autonomous process. With the advent of easier to use machine learning and advanced analytic tools, the dream is to "marry" these two systems together to allow for a truly comprehensive picture of a company's health. The technological capabilities in today's digital era have enabled business intelligence platforms to more effectively combine retrospective analytics of KPIs to incorporate forecasting and the identification of hidden patterns that facilitate multivariate predictive modeling. This chapter will illustrate the complementary link between a data management and mining platform with an e-based visualization api to produce a comprehensive business intelligence application for customer churn (Kudyba, 2014).

Simply put, business intelligence is a blanket term that refers to the processes a company uses to make sense of all their raw data. Every company generates volumes of data through the course of its day, month, quarter, and year. This data can be very simple in nature, such as how many widgets it sold this month, to very complex sentiment data, such as customer reviews of the widgets. Software tools have existed for many decades that allow management to make sense of all this data. These tools often generate aggregated reports or Online Analytical Processing (OLAP) cubes that allow users to view retrospective performance. However these platforms have experienced difficulties in providing real-time reporting or addressing analytics issues, such as what is causing things to occur or what is likely to occur.

Real-time processing is a relatively new initiative for business intelligence. As relational databases become ubiquitous in organizations, new tools facilitate direct connectivity of BI tools into these data repositories and enable management to get an hour-to-hour, day-by-day assessment of various activities. While this allows an organization to quickly understand if a new marketing campaign or product is increasing sales, it still does not allow an organization to predict and make relevant forecasts. Some BI platforms are beginning to utilize various tools to support decision making, incorporating some predictive capabilities; for example, the typical linear regression analysis of sales for each unit or generating what-if scenarios with spreadsheets. The benefits of these tools are that they can quickly export their results into the BI platform and be visualized; there management can review the results and start making better decisions that will affect future outcomes. In essence, they begin to increase their emphasis on predictive analytics. What is needed is a cohesive analytic system that ties this all together by leveraging the visual power of a BI tool, and incorporating KPIs and retrospective analytics with predictive analytics across all facets of the organization to achieve better decision support.

KPIS: AN INDICATION OF PERFORMANCE

BI tools and platforms allow anyone in management to create dynamic dashboards and reports. At the click of a button, reports can be drilled down, reorganized, or aggregated in many different ways. These results are often shared in a visual manner through a server or cube that allows users to quickly log in and see the results. Key performance indicators (KPI) are generally custom metrics that are specific to an industry in which a company operates, and they are usually as simple as measuring the rate of change of sales, overall product quality, or customer satisfaction scores, to name a few. Management keeps these KPIs front and center in their day-to-day operations to pursue strategies to affect these KPIs in a positive manner.

Sometimes these strategies are for a single business unit in a single geographic region, and other times it is corporatewide. Smart corporations use the KPI data to evaluate, propose, and strategize new "go to market" campaigns or sales strategies in an effort to grow revenue or market share. The fallacy with proposing strategies with just KPI data generated from a BI tool is the difficulty in determining whether the new strategy will have the desired results and outcome. The problem is that these KPIs report activity that happened last week, month, or quarter; they present a single metric outcome with no description of what caused the results.

New BI platforms are addressing this issue by investigating initiatives that incorporate more advanced analytics corresponding to KPIs in dashboards.

ADVANCED ANALYTICS

Advanced analytics, or more commonly known as *predictive analytics,* is another umbrella term for extracting information from various data sets to help forecast the future. Techniques range from the popular *linear regression* algorithm to more advanced algorithms such as *gradient boosted trees.*

Usually relegated to the realm of statisticians and computer scientists, and now the data scientist, these robust and advanced analytic techniques are difficult for nonpractitioners to use and understand. While many non-practitioners can understand linear regression, it's very hard to interpret the weight table of a support vector machine. Vast improvements over the years have made these analytic techniques easy to understand for management, but the ability for a nonpractitioner to use these tools—much less interact with them—remains hard to integrate.

The ideal situation is for statisticians/computer scientists (data scientists) to build these analytic models and then make them available in some way within the BI tool. This way nonpractitioners can review the results, interpret them, interact with the model, and even perform what-if simulations by varying the various inputs. As predictive analytics has worked its way into the lexicon of corporations, the need to use these analytics with existing BI tools has become important. Why build a BI dashboard or cube without being able to quickly generate what-if scenarios by varying the inputs.

PRESCRIPTIVE ANALYTICS

Prescriptive analytics is the dynamic application of advanced analytics (AA) and BI in the organization to provide predictive and interactive decision support for strategic initiatives. Once a predictive model has been created, it is then given to the IT group to "put in production."

This is not an optimal situation as it requires IT to "recode" the findings into C++, Java, or some other system that works with existing systems and BI tools within the organization, usually causing a bottleneck in time from the analysis to production phase.

To reduce these bottlenecks, many new advanced analytics tools or platforms readily expose Representational State Transfer (REST) APIs. These are URLs that can be called from a BI tool and execute process in the background to provide the viewer with visual predictive results. A BI user can drill down and create a what-if analysis request, pass it back through the REST API, and instantly get a result. Creating REST APIs suddenly reduces the time from "insight" to "action" for management.

OUR USE CASE

Our use case is related to customer churn and customer up-selling, two typical and important corporate endeavors. Churn seeks to identify the customers who are at risk of leaving, and up-selling is identifying customers who have a propensity to buy more products or services. Both of these use cases are high value, as the cost for keeping existing customers is often lower than finding new customers.

We begin with our data set. The data set is a typical customer data set with various demographic data and locations. We input values of state; mobile usage (in minutes) for 2013 thru 2015; and what service package customers purchased (see Figure 2.1).

The goal is to build an analytic process that identifies customers likely to churn and customers that could be "upsold," too, and then visualizing this information in a popular BI tool. To accomplish this analysis, we use RapidMiner Studio, RapidMiner Server, and Qlik Desktop. RapidMiner studio is a visual programming data science platform; RapidMiner Server creates the REST API; and Qlik Desktop is a popular BI visualization platform. RapidMiner Server acts a facilitator between RapidMiner Studio and Qlik Desktop through REST API. Processes (aka analytic workflows) can be called from Qlik and results quickly visualized.

CHURN AND UP-SELL ANALYTIC PROCESS

The analytic design of the churn and up-sell model is done in RapidMiner Studio. Users navigate RapidMiner Studio by dragging and dropping "operators" and chaining them together. Each operator has a specific task, and when several of them are chained together it's called a process (see Figure 2.2). The process involves data selection, transformations, and the application of mining techniques.

The churn and up-sell modeling are both done in a single process inside RapidMiner Studio, as shown previously. The analytics are executed and modeled whenever Qlik calls them, and then visualized in a custom dashboard. The intermediate step, exposing this process as callable REST API, is not shown as it's a simple URL that's embedded inside the Qlik dashboard configuration files. An example URL could be http://rmus-tott:8080/api/rest/process/Qlik%20Churn%20Demo, for illustrative purposes only.

When this URL is pinged from a browser, it retrieves the staged results and provides them with the unmodeled raw data that will be used as inputs for the advanced analytic process as an HTML table as shown in Figure 2.3.

THE QLIK DASHBOARD

Qlik Desktop and other similar BI tools (i.e., Tableau) allow users to build custom dashboards across the organization. Dashboards and reports can easily be built in ad hoc fashion and provide drill down capabilities into data. In normal situations, they are merely connected to the organization's data store. In this example, the data is connected to the organization's data

ExampleSet (4793 examples, 0 special attributes, 14 regular attributes)

Filter (4,793 / 4,793 examples): all

Row No.	State	Mobile 2015	Mobile 2014	Mobile 2013	Land 2015	Land 2014	Land 2013	Age	Pack	Limited serv...	Blocked ser...	Customer_id	Churn Status
1	AL	41.260	42.470	30.143	19.557	20.433	23.673	58	P1	0	0	1259443438	Loyal
2	AL	14.160	21.560	79.523	14.590	17.813	19.547	42	P3	1	0	1227726347	Loyal
3	AL	129.693	118.983	70.800	12.890	18.280	16.573	49	P2	1	0	832873945	Loyal
4	AL	110.130	101.357	122.143	34.683	36.533	43.827	53	P1	0	0	750978468	Churn
5	AL	60.670	63.383	105.503	54.140	59.923	55.387	69	P1	1	0	1679498513	?
6	AL	47.387	57.340	16.010	17.830	18.570	12.337	63	P3	1	0	1353687242	Loyal
7	AL	78.803	23.687	44.977	62.190	62.753	69.733	40	P1	0	0	1426106648	Loyal
8	AL	57.957	33.530	19.450	57.020	64.237	65.773	43	P1	0	0	1193076574	Loyal
9	AL	39.940	24.630	50.280	46.230	56.770	56.057	52	P3	1	0	988023348	Loyal
10	AL	51.427	56.313	82.573	35.113	30.373	35.290	50	P2	0	0	1071445269	?
11	AL	95.427	81.160	66.300	50.837	55.417	49.190	24	P1	1	0	1732975435	Loyal
12	AL	49.547	25.760	27.990	17.050	14.870	21.280	34	P2	0	0	1897725692	Loyal
13	AL	79.657	26.427	52.623	20.037	23.137	15.340	51	P1	1	0	2069397211	Loyal
14	AL	108.703	30.600	33.090	50.743	56.437	47.783	56	P2	0	0	162448491	Loyal
15	AL	81.573	86.103	19.923	66.310	61.277	57.310	56	P1	1	0	1464422302	?
16	AL	50.463	19.497	76.373	35.110	39.333	30.453	64	P1	1	0	114696718	Loyal
17	AL	33.863	25.890	67.630	63.287	58.960	58.427	25	P1	1	0	1901960929	Loyal
18	Al	130.013	44.027	23.377	42.593	44.970	41.377	38	P1	0	0	1421507337	Loyal

Figure 2.1   Raw data (RapidMiner, 2016).

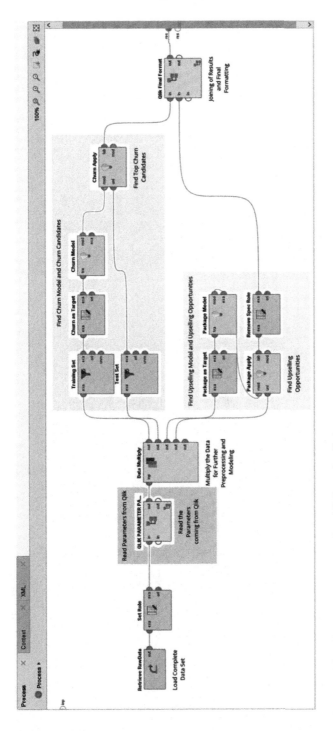

Figure 2.2 Chaining operators (RapidMiner Studio).

State	Age	Pack	Limited service (one way)	Blocked service (two way)	ChurnStatus	Gender	Mobile	Land	prediction(Pack)	Customer_id (id)	prediction(ChurnStatus) (prediction)	ChurnConfidence	PackOffer
AL	58	P1	0	0	Loyal	Male	41.260	19.557	P1	1259443438	2	2	
AL	42	P3	1	0	Loyal	Female	14.160	14.590	P1	1227726347	2	2	
AL	49	P2	1	0	Loyal	Female	129.693	12.890	P1	832873945	2	2	
AL	53	P1	0	0	Churn	Male	110.130	34.683	P1	7509780468	2	2	
AL	69	P1	1	0	2	Male	60.670	54.140	P1	16794998513	Loyal	0	
AL	63	P3	1	0	Loyal	Female	47.387	17.830	P1	1353687242	2	2	
AL	40	P1	0	0	Loyal	Female	78.803	62.190	P1	1426106648	2	2	
AL	43	P1	0	0	Loyal	Male	57.957	57.020	P1	1193076574	2	2	
AL	52	P3	0	0	Loyal	Male	39.940	16.230	P1	9880023348	2	2	
AL	50	P2	1	0	2	Female	51.427	35.113	P1	10714455269	Churn	1	
AL	24	P1	0	0	Loyal	Female	95.427	50.837	P1	1732975435	2	2	
AL	34	P2	0	0	Loyal	Female	49.547	17.050	P1	1897725692	2	2	
AL	51	P1	1	0	Loyal	Female	79.657	20.037	P1	2069397211	2	2	
AL	56	P2	0	0	2	Male	108.703	50.743	P1	16248491	Loyal	0	
AL	58	P1	1	0	Loyal	Female	81.573	86.310	P1	1464422302	2	2	
AL	64	P1	1	0	Loyal	Female	50.463	35.110	P1	114696718	2	2	
AL	25	P1	1	0	Loyal	Female	33.863	63.287	P1	19019609929	2	2	
AL	38	P1	0	0	Loyal	Female	130.013	42.593	P1	1421502337	2	2	
AL	69	P3	2	2	Loyal	Male	92.580	23.663	P1	974667229	2	2	
AL	23	P3	3	2	2	Male	149.450	36.933	P1	1807280552	Loyal	0.043	P1
AL	35	P1	1	0	Loyal	Male	116.077	6.690	P1	13238997796	2	2	
AL	28	P2	1	2	Loyal	Male	57.373	55.607	P1	1301465386	2	2	
AL	62	P3	4	2	Loyal	Male	62.840	5.237	P1	12982206153	2	2	
AL	70	P2	2	0	Loyal	Female	192.293	46.480	P1	828490189	2	2	
AL	40	P2	2	0	2	Female	31.210	41.057	P1	2020126361	Loyal	0.043	P1
AL	47	P1	3	3	Churn	Female	28.337	36.567	P1	903535261	2	2	
AL	59	P1	4	1	Loyal	Female	7.137	47.543	P1	1824074545	2	2	

Figure 2.3 HTML table.

store, but is fed first through the RapidMiner process and then loaded into the dashboard you see in Figure 2.4.

For our use case, an end user has already built a dashboard with a heat map of U.S. states that can be filtered according to KPIs. The dashboard also includes a fact table, which depicts the underlying data of metrics according to dimensional attributes, and finally color coded KPIs. The KPIs in this case involve average churn rate, average age, and average limited service with the ability to toggle through the years. Any end user can click on a state a drill down to these KPIs.

However, if users wish to better understand the attributes of the populations who are likely to churn or who are good candidates for cross sell initiatives, they can navigate to the second dashboard via the API, called Prediction, where they will be presented with the overall churn prediction across the United States (red bars), and selected state churn predictions (yellow bars). Marketing and sales departments can easily see what the key characteristics of age, gender, and service statistics are that have been analyzed and tested in a robust manner to make fact-based decisions for new campaigns. This second dashboard (Figure 2.5) contains the mined data with the RapidMiner server that performed the advanced analytics, which incorporates statistically and algorithm-based analytics to produce likelihoods and probabilities according to multivariate attributes.

If users navigate to the action dashboard, they can see what potential upsell opportunities are for a particular customer in a state. Now the organization can confidently make new marketing campaigns in a selected region, while driving new sales from up-sell opportunities.

CONCLUSION

As a company generates new data and as customers' spending habits change, the models built in RapidMiner Studio just need to be retrained with new data. The Qlik end users do not see this retraining, nor do they need to interact with it. They just consume the results and make decisions proactively to reduce customer churn and drive new sales from up-sell opportunities.

The ultimate result is more robust decision support for the end user, who now can quickly understand what is happening through retrospective metrics and visuals, and then take the next step of leveraging the more actionable information of what is likely to happen, which is produced and made available through the application described.

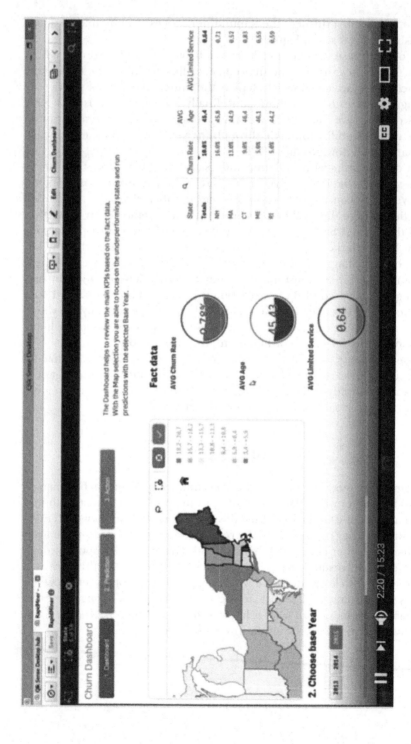

Figure 2.4 A traditional dashboard.

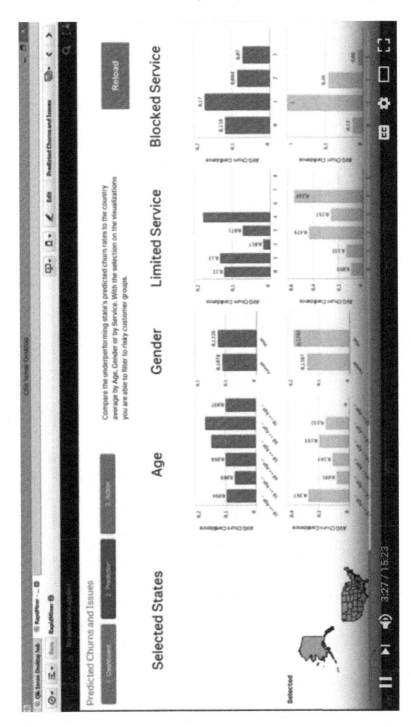

Figure 2.5 Dashboard incorporating advanced analytics.

REFERENCE

Kudyba, S. (2014). *Big data, mining and analytics: Components of strategic decision making*. New York, NY: Taylor Francis.

CHAPTER 3

PREDICTIVE ANALYTICAL MODEL OF THE CEO COMPENSATION OF MAJOR U.S. CORPORATE INSURANCE COMPANIES

Kenneth Lawrence
New Jersey Institute of Technology

Gary Kleinman
Montclair State University

Sheila Lawrence
Rutgers University

ABSTRACT

This research focuses on the development of a predictive regression model to investigate the relationship of CEO compensation of U.S. corporate insurance companies to other companies' financial status and profitability, a forecasting model was developed, based on 2014 corporate data. This forecasting model was used to forecast the 2015 compensation of each of the CEOs.

Most large U.S. companies use peer groups to gauge their CEO pay. Peer groups are used for benchmarking that is arranged to reflect the target levels in major ways. Peers usually include close competitors, as well as companies of similar size and stature.

The performance of the companies is typically measured by accounting and financial ratios as return on equity, return on assets, and stock market returns. Although accounting and financial ratios provide important information the companies use for benchmarking, they usually do not net out the effects of differences in exogenous, company specific conditions that may affect company value, although they are many times beyond the CEO's control.

Federal securities' laws require clear, concise and understandable disclosures about compensation paid to CEOs of public companies. In the annual proxy statement, a company must disclose information concerning the amount and type of compensation paid to its chief executive officer. A company also must disclose the criteria used in reaching executive compensation decisions and the relationship between the compensation practices and the corporation. To determine the CEO's compensation, a regression model can be used to predict total compensation based on the firm's performance and industry. The regression model in effect proffers the benchmarking criterion to use in determining the target company CEO's executive compensation

PREDICTIVE REGRESSION MODELS FOR THE CEO COMPENSATION OF THE INSURANCE VERSUS CORPORATE COMPANIES

Based on the development of a predictive regression model to investigate the relationship of CEO compensation of U.S. corporate insurance companies to the companies' financial status and profitability, a forecasting model was developed based on 2014 corporate data (Bulan, Sanyal, & Yen, 2010; Eckles, Halek, He, Sommer, & Zhang, 1992; Mayers & Smith, 1992; Sun, Wei, & Huang, 2013; Wilson & Higgins, 2008). This forecasting model was then used to forecast the 2015 compensation of each of the CEOs.

Best subsets regression was used to identify the model that best predicted the CEO compensation. Best subsets regression is a systematic approach used to select the explanatory variables that best explain the dependent variable, thus indicating which explanatory variables to include in the forecasting multiple regression equation. Best subsets regression is simply a collection of the best regression analyses. The statistical program presents the output of different subsets of the predictive explanatory variables. The best fitting regression model can be then selected based on R^2 values, adjusted R^2 values, and the Mallows C_p statistic. The best subsets regression maximizes R^2 and adjusted R^2 values and minimizes the C_p statistic.

The modeling structure includes several variables (Table 3.1).

Data for each company were retried from various sources, including the Mergent database; inspection of corporate website investor relations areas, which often provide corporate Securities and Exchange Commission filing; as well as other information and documents filed by the sample firms with the SEC.gov website (e.g., Forms 10-K, the so-called corporate annual report; Forms 10-Q, the so-called corporate quarterly report; and proxy statements). All statements presented in foreign currency were translated to U.S. currency using the foreign currency to U.S. dollar conversion factor available at the date of the cited report.

TABLE 3.1	Variables of Modeling Structure
Variable	**Title**
Y	CEO compensation
X_1	Total corporate return
X_2	Corporate price earning
X_3	Number of Morningstars for the corporation
X_4	Corporate revenue
X_5	Operating income
X_6	Net income
X_7	Operating cash flow
X_8	Capital spending
X_9	Free cash-flow
X_{10}	Dividends per share
X_{11}	Book value per share
X_{12}	Shares outstanding
X_{13}	Return on equity
X_{14}	Return on assets
X_{15}	Net margin
X_{16}	Asset turnover
X_{17}	Financial leverage
X_{18}	Operating merger
X_{19}	Long term debt
X_{20}	Total equity
X_{21}	Fixed assets

U.S. INSURANCE COMPANIES

The corporate insurance companies used in this study included:

AIG
Chubb
Manulife
UnitedHealth
MetLife
Allstate
CNA
SunLife
Principal Finances
Progressive
Aflac
Hartford Finances
Aegon
PRU
Aetna
Anthem

Table 3.2 shows in the left-hand column the insurance companies that made up the sample used here, with the percentage deviation of the CEOs' actual compensation from the forecasted compensation for 2015. This latter result is shown in the right-hand column.

The regression prediction model is the following:

$$Y = 3740518 + 60.1X_5 + 278X_8 + 6704X_9 - 179X_{10} + \qquad (3.1)$$
$$3269773X_{11} + 5074833X_1 - 423X_{21}$$

The model's R^2 is 66.38%. The model was built using Minitab 17.2's best-subsets regression variable selections and the model was constructed using Minitab 17.2 multiple regression. The compensation model was built around 2014 data to make predictions into the year 2015. Seven of the 21 variables proved significant predictors of CEO compensation. The successful predictor variables were operating income, capital spending, dividends per share, free cash flow, financial leverage, book value per share, and fixed assets. The high R^2 demonstrates the utility of the best set regression routine for understanding the determinants of CEO pay in the insurance industry.

Board of directors' compensation committees should consider the use of such a model built on industry-relevant data in determining appropriate compensation for CEOs in the insurance and related industries.

TABLE 3.2 Percentage Error Between 2015 CEO Forecasting Model of Actual CEO Compensation	
Company	Percentage (%)
AIG	10.0
Chubb	2.7
Manulife	7.8
UnitedHealth	−21.2
MetLife	−4.3
Allstate	9.9
CNA	5.3
SunLife	0.1
Principal Finances	−3.1
Progressive	−4.8
Aflac	2.3
Hartford Finances	−9.3
Aegon	10.1
PRU	2.3
Aetna	−0.1
Anthem	0.1

REFERENCES

Bulan, L., Sanyal, P., & Yen, Z. (2010). A few bad apples: An analysis of CEO performance pay and firm productivity. *Journal of Economics and Business, 62,* 273–306.

Eckles, D. L., Halek, M., He, E., Sommer, D. W., & Zhang, R. (1992) Earnings smoothing, executive compensation and corporate governance: Evidence from the property and liability insurance industry. *Journal of Risk and Insurance, 78,* 761–790.

Mayers, D., & Smith, C. (1992). Executive compensation in life insurance industry. *Journals of Business, 65,* 1.

Sun, F., Wei, X., & Huang, X. (2013). CEO performance and firm performance evidence from U.S. property and liability insurance industries. *Review of Accounting and Finance, 12*(3), 252–278.

Wilson, A., & Higgins, E. (2008). CEO pay/performance sensitivity in the insurance industry. *Journal of Insurance Issues, 24,* 1–16.

SECTION II

BUSINESS APPLICATIONS

CHAPTER 4

ANALYZING OPERATIONAL AND FINANCIAL PERFORMANCE OF U.S. HOSPITALS USING TWO-STAGE PRODUCTION PROCESS

Dinesh Pai
Pennsylvania State University, Harrisburg

Hengameh Hosseini
Pennsylvania State University, Harrisburg

ABSTRACT

We determine whether hospitals that have better operational efficiency also exhibit better financial performance. Utilizing data envelopment analysis (DEA), we examine the performance of 90 U.S. hospitals for the year 2013 via a two-stage hospital production process that evaluates operational performance in the first stage and financial performance in the second. The effect of hospital location and size on operational and financial performance

Contemporary Perspectives on Data Mining, Volume 3, pages 49–65
Copyright © 2018 by Information Age Publishing
All rights of reproduction in any form reserved.

was revealed by evaluating technical and scale efficiencies. Relatively few of the hospitals were efficient in financial performance compared with their efficiency in operational performance. Only a few hospitals were efficient in both stages, which suggests that a few hospitals are able to efficiently generate profits from their operations. In both stages, the majority of the hospitals were found to be in decreasing returns to scale (DRS). Furthermore, DRS was found among most of the hospitals, irrespective of their size and location in both stages. The results provide important insights to governments, insurers, and employers, especially those struggling with rising healthcare costs, who are increasingly looking to purchase care from efficient and low-cost producers.

U.S. hospitals are facing tremendous pressure to reduce healthcare costs and provide better access to care without lowering the quality of care so as to meet the aims of the Affordable Care Act. Several factors such as the volume shift from inpatient to outpatient visits, an increasing emphasis on value-based purchasing, intensifying competition, reimbursement reductions, costly new technology, among other factors, combined with declining occupancy, have significantly reduced operating margins (Sultz & Young, 2009; Weil, 2011), a measure of hospital financial performance. Notwithstanding these challenges, hospitals are increasingly being held accountable for their operational and financial performance, which are of interest to health insurers, government authorities, communities, and hospital management itself. Obviously, a better understanding of the relationship between operational and financial performance can provide the key for improving hospital performance.

There exists a broad literature by both academics and practitioners devoted to measuring hospital efficiency and productivity (Hollingsworth, 2008). Hundreds of hospital efficiency studies have found evidence that there is significant operational (technical) inefficiency in the U.S. and other health systems (Chilingerian & Sherman, 2011). While several approaches—such as ratio analysis, combined utilization and productivity analysis, statistical production, and cost functions—have been used to measure hospital performance and efficiency, data envelopment analysis (DEA) "has become the researchers' method of choice for finding best practices and evaluating productive inefficiency," according to Chilingerian and Sherman (2011).

DEA, a mathematical programming approach for characterizing the relationships among multiple inputs and multiple outputs, estimates best practices frontier and allows the measurement of relative efficiency levels. The popularity of DEA in efficiency studies is due in part to its flexibility, which is essential to the evaluation of complex organizations such as hospitals. Myriad applications of DEA have appeared in the hospital productivity and efficiency literature. Hollingsworth (2003, 2008) provides an excellent review of the past literature. However, few studies have applied

DEA to investigate the financial performance of hospitals; and despite the increasing emphasis on efficiency and quality, evidently just a few studies have considered quality measure in DEA efficiency studies (Clement, Valdmanis, Bazzoli, Zhao, & Chukmaitov, 2008; Nayar, Ozcan, & Nguyen, 2013; Valdmanis, Rosko, & Mutter, 2008).

Most hospital performance studies employ labor (physicians, registered nurses, and other personnel), capital (staffed beds), and, in a few cases supply cost, equipment expense, and operating expenses as inputs; and for outputs they use inpatient days, surgeries, outpatient visits, emergency visits, adjusted discharges, and in a few cases, different measures of quality. While these inputs and outputs can characterize a hospital's operational performance, they do not reflect the financial performance of a hospital. In our view, to evaluate hospital financial performance one must account for additional factors, such as net patient revenue and operating margin in a DEA analysis. By incorporating some new factors in a two-stage approach, we explore the operational and financial performance of 90 Pennsylvania hospitals.

In this study, we define a two-stage hospital production process that generates operational performance in the first stage and financial performance in the second. The effect of location and hospital size on operational and financial performance is elucidated by evaluating both technical and scale efficiencies. In operational performance, we find decreasing returns to scale (DRS) among the hospitals. In financial performance, however, the hospitals exhibit increasing returns to scale (IRS). Both rural and urban hospitals exhibit DRS in operational performance and IRS in financial performance.

LITERATURE REVIEW

Quality of care in U.S. hospitals has been a growing concern ever since the Institute of Medicine's (IOM) landmark reports (*To Err Is Human,* 1999: *Crossing the Quality Chasm,* 2001) revealed the widespread incidence of medical errors and substandard care. Due to preventable medical errors, hospitals incurred estimated total costs of between $17 billion and $29 billion per year (Kohn, Corrigan, & Donaldson 1999). Despite the growing concern about quality of care, there are not many studies in the hospital efficiency literature that have incorporated quality. In a report prepared for the Agency of Healthcare Research and Quality in 2008, McGlynn (2008) observed that virtually none of the efficiency measures used in the literature included the quality dimension. This gap in the literature could be attributed to the fact that quality is difficult to define and quantify. In the manufacturing industry, the definition of quality and the instruments for measuring quality have been developed and are widely used; however, characteristics such as the intangibility, simultaneity, and heterogeneity of services in industry in general, and healthcare services in particular, make defining and measuring quality very challenging. The problem is further exacerbated by the necessary reliance on subjective patient perceptions. In the recent past, however, researchers have incorporated different measures of quality in their efficiency studies. In this chapter, we review relevant literature pertaining to hospital efficiency studies. Clement et al. (2008) evaluated DEA models of hospital efficiency using desirable output (patient stays) and undesirable output (risk-adjusted patient mortality). They found that lower technical efficiency is associated with poorer risk-adjusted quality outcomes in the study hospitals. Applying a two-stage DEA process, the authors found that quality of care could be improved by increasing the number of labor inputs in low-quality hospitals. Furthermore, high quality hospitals tended to have slack on personnel. Using a sample of Virginia hospitals, Nayar and Ozcan (2008) incorporated three process quality measures in their DEA model. The authors found a high correlation between efficiency models with and without quality measures. They noted that the technically efficient hospitals were also found to be efficiently producing the quality outputs.

More recently, using a sample of 1,074 U.S. hospitals, Ferrier and Trivitt (2013) compared a variety of DEA quality indices and a DEA variety of efficiency models to determine how the treatment of quality influenced findings regarding technical efficiency. They concluded that outcome quality measures had a greater impact on technical efficiency than process quality measures. Nayar et al. (2013), using slack-based additive DEA models in 371 urban acute care hospitals, found that less than 20% of the sample hospitals were optimally performing for both quality and efficiency. Furthermore, they found that public, small, teaching hospitals had higher DEA efficiency and quality scores. Chowdhury, Zelenyuk, Laporte, & Wodchis (2014) compared productivity, efficiency and technological changes with and without case-mix as output categories using panel data on Ontario hospitals for the period 2002–2006 and found that productivity, efficiency and technological changes were significantly different between two alternative models.

We have built on the previous literature on hospital efficiency and quality of care in hospitals by using recent developments in DEA literature and by using broad-based outcome quality measures. The objective of this study was twofold: first, using a two-stage hospital production process that generates operational performance in the first stage and financial performance in the second, we determined whether hospitals that had better operational performance also had better financial performance. Second, we included two measures of quality variables—readmission and mortality index—as intermediate factors to investigate their impact on hospital efficiency.

CONCEPTUAL FRAMEWORK, DATA, AND VARIABLES

Conceptual Model

Health economics literature treats a hospital as a healthcare producing "firm," thereby lending itself to efficiency analysis. However, characteristics such as the intangibility, simultaneity, and heterogeneity of healthcare services make the hospital's production process inherently complex. Unlike manufacturing systems, hospitals operate as open systems, and are thereby exposed to demand variations. For example, hospitals produce hundreds or even thousands of outputs: there are over 500 diagnosis related groups (DRGs), and each output differs by individual patient as to the degree of disease severity and complexity required for treatment (Gaynor, Kleiner, & Vogt, 2014).

Hospital complexity affects effective measurement of hospital production, which consequently impedes efficiency analysis. The difficulty in analyzing hospital production is evident in that despite a large literature on hospital performance evaluation, according to Chilingerian and Sherman (2011), "Rarely have two researchers studied the same problem and when they have, rarely have they employed the same categories of inputs and outputs." The literature proposes several reasons for this disparity: (a) ability to adequately control for the types of patients and severity of illnesses treated at a hospital (Newhouse, 1994); (b) output aggregation, especially for larger hospitals that provide a broader range of services and specialized treatments that are often more costly, may result in incorrectly measure scope of output (Gaynor, Kleiner, & Vogt, 2014); and (c) availability of an easily accessible dataset and the desired variables.

Figure 4.1 describes the hospital production process, which is divided into two stages and 10 factors that are expressed as inputs and outputs as shown in this figure. Stage 1 measures operational performance (or

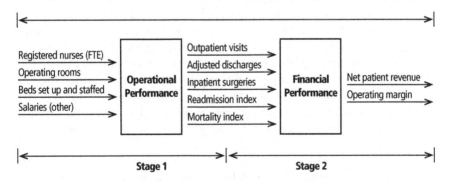

Figure 4.1 Hospital production process (two-stage).

technical efficiency), i.e., a hospital's ability to generate patient visits and quality outcomes in terms of its labor, capital, and salaries (other). Stage 2 measures financial performance, i.e., a hospital's ability to generate net patient revenues and operating margin in terms of its patient visits and quality outcomes.

Data Collection

To test our suggested two-stage model of the hospital production process shown in Figure 4.1, we used the 2013 data for Pennsylvania acute care hospitals, which comes from the Pennsylvania Health Care Cost Containment Council's (PHC4) Hospital Performance Reports And Financial Analysis Reports, augmented by the CMS Hospital Cost Reports (HCR). Data was available for 143 hospitals. Seventeen hospitals in the HCR for which case mix indexes were missing were also excluded. Our sample included only those hospitals that had positive operating margins; 90 hospitals met this criterion. Although we could have increased the number of hospitals in our sample by invoking the translation invariance property of DEA (Ali & Seiford, 1990) to allow negative values for operating margin, such use is restricted to the convex case, and some properties, e.g., returns to scale (RTS), were not translation invariant.

Input and Output Variables

Previous studies and deliberations with practitioners formed the basis for selecting a specific set of inputs and outputs for our DEA model. We selected four inputs: Number of beds set up and staffed (BEDSSS) and operating rooms (TOTORM) as the proxy for capital, full-time equivalent registered nurses (RNUFTE) as a proxy for labor, and other salaries (SALOTH), which included salaries of all hospital employees barring the salaries of registered nurses. Operating rooms, while a great source of revenue, are also among the costliest elements of hospitals (Elixhauser & Andrews, 2010). In 2011, over 15 million operating room (OR) procedures were performed in U.S. hospitals (Weiss & Elixhauser, 2014). These procedures—often life-saving—rely on the latest in surgical technology and sophisticated diagnostic equipment, which are capital investments. Registered nurses (RNUFTE), on average, formed a significant proportion (28%) of the total employees among the hospitals in our dataset.

The variables outpatient visits (OUTPAT), inpatient surgeries (SURINP), and total operating revenues (TOPREV) served as intermediate factors in the sense they are outputs from the first stage and inputs to the second stage. The PHC4 database did not include data on total outpatient visits; hence, as a proxy for total outpatient visits, we aggregated outpatient visits to cardiac catheterization laboratory, imaging centers (CT scan and MRI scan), diagnostic and therapeutic nuclear medicine centers, diagnostic and therapeutic radiology, and outpatient surgeries. Net patient revenues (NPAREV) and operating margins (OPEMAR) were the outputs from the second stage and represented a hospital's ability to generate revenue and profit in terms of its current labor, capital, and other operating expenses.

We included two measures of quality in our model: readmission index and mortality index, which measure outcome quality and are weighted averages of risk-adjusted readmissions rate (RAR) and risk-adjusted mortality rate (RAM), respectively, for 11 common medical procedures and treatments identified by ICD-9-CM (International Classification of Diseases, Ninth Revision, Clinical Modification) codes for hospitals in Pennsylvania. The following procedures and treatments were used: abnormal heartbeat, chest pain, chronic obstructive pulmonary disease, congestive heart failure, diabetes, gallbladder removal, heart attack, hypotension, kidney disease, pneumonia, and stroke.

$$\text{Morality Index}_h = \frac{\sum c_{ph} \text{RAM}_{ph}}{C_h} \ \forall h; \qquad (4.1)$$

$$\text{Readmission Index}_h = \frac{\sum c_{ph} \text{RAR}_{ph}}{C_h} \ \forall h \qquad (4.2)$$

Mortality Index$_h$ captures the risk-adjusted mortality rate from the pth procedure for the hth hospital. Similarly, Readmission Index$_h$ captures the risk-adjusted readmission rate from the pth procedure for the hth hospital; c_{ph} captures number of cases in pth procedure for the hth hospital. C_h captures the total number of cases across all of the 11 procedures. Since both indices are undesirable intermediate variables; that is, we would like to reduce both readmissions and mortality, we included in our models: (1-Mortality Index$_h$) and (1-Readmission Index$_h$, respectively. Table 4.1 provides the descriptive statistics for our variables.

METHODS AND RESULTS

In this section, we analyze the operation efficiency and financial performance of 90 hospitals using DEA. DEA was first proposed by Charnes, Cooper, and Rhodes (1978), and since its conception it has been greatly developed and extended. For an introduction to the basic DEA models and theoretical extensions, we refer the reader to Cooper, Seiford, and Tone

TABLE 4.1 Descriptive Statistics		
Variables	Mean	*SD*
Inputs		
Registered Nurses (FTE)	535.58	594.27
Number of Operating Rooms	13.79	12.39
Beds	266.74	241.09
Salaries (Excluding RN salaries)	107.01	138.71
Intermediate Factors		
Adjusted Discharges	21,422.96	23,496.88
Adjusted Surgeries	24,439.79	28,728.01
Outpatient Visits	116,022.48	87,162.16
Readmission Index	13.50	9.82
Mortality Index	2.56	2.11
Outputs		
Net Patient Revenue[a]	$299.02	$378.09
Operating Margin (%)	6.51	5.40

[a] Millions of dollars

(2000). The technique is based on the empirical estimation of a frontier through the application of a mathematical programming model to the observed data. This frontier identifies the most efficient combinations of inputs and outputs.

Most studies in hospital efficiency literature use an input-oriented DEA approach, based on the argument that hospitals, especially community hospitals, cannot choose their level of output, which depends on demand for health services. Some have used an output-oriented approach (Chirikos & Sear, 2000; Ozcan & Bannick, 1994), while other studies have applied both input- and output-oriented approaches to the same dataset (Burgess & Wilson, 1996; Chirikos & Sear, 2000). Coelli and Perelman (1999) demonstrated the existence of a strong degree of correlation between the input- and output-oriented results for many instances. The choice of orientation, however, depends on the objective of production units under relevant production and management constraints (Nguyen & Coelli, 2009). In this study, we apply the output-oriented approach, which involves adjusting output levels while holding inputs and technology constant. The output orientation was selected because we sought to maximize the number of patient days, outpatient visits, surgeries, and outcome quality that could be produced given the inputs available.

The CCR (Charnes, Cooper, & Rhode, 1978) or constant returns to scale (CRS) output-oriented DEA model given here is employed to measure the efficiency in operations and financial performance (Charnes et al., 1978) to enable us to find efficient points on the frontier:

$$\max \phi_o^t + \varepsilon \left\{ \sum_{k=1}^{m} s_k^- + \sum_{i=1}^{r} s_i^+ \right\} t = 1,2;$$

$$s.t. \sum_{j=1}^{n} x_{kj} \lambda_j + s_k^- = x_{ko}, \quad k = 1,\ldots,m;$$

$$\sum_{j=1}^{n} y_{ij} \lambda_j - s_i^+ = \phi_o^t y_{io}, \quad i = 1,\ldots,r;$$

$$\lambda_j, s_k^-, s_i^+ \geq 0,$$

(4.1)

where x_{kj} and y_{ij} are the amount of the kth input consumed and the amount of the ith output produced by the jth DMU (or hospital), respectively. Parameter ε is an infinitesimal constant (a non-Archimedean quantity). In Stage 1 ($t = 1$), we have $k = 4$ inputs – registered nurses (FTE), beds set up and staffed, total operating rooms, and other operating expenses, and $i = 4$ outputs – outpatient visits, adjusted inpatient days, inpatient surgeries and total operating revenues. In Stage 2 ($t = 2$), we have $k = 4$ inputs – outpatient visits, adjusted inpatient days, inpatient surgeries and total operating revenues, and $i = 2$ outputs – net patient revenue and operating margin.

Let ϕ_o^1 and ϕ_o^2 be the optimal values for (1) Stage 1 and Stage 2 models, respectively. The output-oriented CCR model is efficient if and only if any optimal solution of (1) satisfies (a) $\phi_o^t = 1$, (b) all slacks s_k^{-*}, s_i^{+*} $k = 1,\ldots,m$, $i = 1,\ldots,r$, are zero. Thus, if $\phi_o^1 = 1$ and all input/output slacks are zero, then a hospital is said to be CCR efficient in operations; if $\phi_o^2 = 1$ and all input/output slacks are zero, then a hospital is said to be CCR efficient in financial performance.

As most previous studies have employed an input-oriented approach, in order to test the robustness of our results with respect to orientation, we first obtained efficiency scores for each stage using an input-oriented CCR model, which assumes constant-returns-to-scale (CRS). Then, we obtained efficiency scores for each stage using the BCC model (2; Banker, Charnes, & Cooper, 1984) with both input and output orientation. The BCC model assumes variable-returns-to-scale (VRS) model. Note that input and output orientations produce identical technical efficiency in case of CRS frontier.

$$\max \gamma_o' + \varepsilon \left\{ \sum_{k=1}^{m} s_k^- + \sum_{i=1}^{r} s_i^+ \right\} \quad t = 1, 2;$$

$$\text{s.t.} \sum_{j=1}^{n} x_{kj} \lambda_j + s_k^- = x_{ko}, \quad k = 1, \ldots, m; \tag{4.2}$$

$$\sum_{j=1}^{n} \lambda_j = 1;$$

$$\lambda_j, s_k^-, s_i^+ \geq 0$$

Let γ_o^1 and γ_o^2 be the optimal values for (1) Stage 1 and Stage 2 models, respectively. Define a scale efficiency measure by $\pi_o^t = \phi_o^{t*}/\gamma_o^{t*}$, for $t = 1, 2$. Obviously, $\pi_o^t \geq 1$. If $\pi_o^t = 1$, a hospital is called scale-efficient; otherwise, if $\pi_o^t > 1$, a hospital is called scale-inefficient. For a hospital to be called scale efficient $\pi_o^t = 1$, which is possible if and only if $\gamma_o^{t*} = \phi_o^{t*}$.

The Wilcoxon matched pairs signed-rank sum test results suggest that there is not a statistically significant difference between input-oriented and output-oriented models, which indicates that the models generate similar mean efficiency scores under output and input orientations in the case of VRS frontier.

Furthermore, Wilcoxon matched pairs signed-rank sum test to determine the relationship between CCR models, with and without quality measures, for both stages revealed that there was a difference between the models, which was statistically significant ($p = 0.000$). The results were similar for the BCC models. Table 4.2 reports the efficiency scores for the previous models.

A clear trend that emerges from the efficiency scores in Table 4.2 is that fewer hospitals were efficient in Stage 2 compared with hospitals in Stage 1, which suggests that only a few hospitals were able to efficiently generate profits from their operations. For instance, when quality measures were included, three hospitals—Gettysburg, Barnes Kasson County ,and Troy Community—were efficient in both dimensions of operations

TABLE 4.2 CCR Efficiency Scores	Without Quality Measures		With Quality Measures	
	Stage 1	Stage 2	Stage 1	Stage 2
Number of efficient DMUs	20	6	26	13
Mean	1.23	1.66	1.13	1.54
Standard Deviation	0.33	0.49	0.15	0.46
% efficient	22.22	6.67	28.89	14.44

and profitability; only one hospital, Hospital of the University of Pennsylvania, was efficient in both dimensions with and without the inclusion of quality measures.

Overall, 29% of the hospitals were efficiently operating under operational performance (Stage 1) and only 14% under financial performance (Stage 2). Potential improvements of 13% in intermediate factors are indicated for nearly 71% of the hospitals, and 54% improvement in net patient revenue and operating margin is expected for approximately 86% of the hospitals. On average, hospitals had a relatively better performance with respect to operational performance.

Scale Efficiency

Scale efficiency has long been recognized in the hospital literature as an important issue, and has been widely discussed in DEA studies pertaining to the hospital performance evaluation literature (Banker, Conrad, & Strauss, 1986; Ferrier & Valdmanis, 1996; Valdmanis, Rosko, & Mutter, 2008). However, the CCR model assumes CRS production technology, which implies that any proportional change in every input usage would result in the same proportional change in every output. In order to determine the scale efficiency of the 90 hospitals, we employ the output-oriented VRS DEA model (2).

Only those hospitals that were CRS efficient are scale-efficient. The Wilcoxon signed rank sum test was applied to CRS and VRS scores in each stage. The results were significant ($p < 0.001$), indicating that a serious scale inefficiency was present for the 90 hospitals in both operational performance and financial performance. We next determined whether increasing or decreasing returns to scale (IRS or DRS) was the primary cause of scale inefficiency.

According to Banker, Charnes, & Cooper (1984), the optimal solution for λ_j^* ($j = 1, \ldots, n$) in (1), i.e., the magnitude of $\sum_{j=1}^{n} \lambda_j^*$, contains the information for RTS classification. Banker and Thrall (1992), however, discuss the possibility of multiple optimal solutions for λ_j^* for (1), which may lead to misclassification of DMUs with respect to RTS by $\sum_{j=1}^{n} \lambda_j^*$. To avoid the misclassification, we used the result of Zhu and Sen (1995) to determine the RTS classification. That is, let DMU_o be a hospital under evaluation and λ_j^* be an optimal solution to (1) associated with ϕ_o^{t*}, then CRS prevail for DMU_o if and only if $\gamma_o^{t*} = \phi_o^{t*}$, i.e., $\pi_o^t = 1$; otherwise, if $\gamma_o^{t*} \neq \phi_o^{t*}$, i.e., $\pi_o^t > 1$, then IRS prevail for DMU_o if and only if $\sum_{j=1}^{n} \lambda_j^* < 1$, and DRS prevail for DMU_o if and only if $\sum_{j=1}^{n} \lambda_j^* > 1$.

The distribution of returns-to-scale (RTS) for each of the stages showed that approximately, 26 hospitals were scale efficient in operational performance, whereas only 13 hospitals were scale efficient in financial performance. In operational performance, among the scale inefficient hospitals, an increasingly high proportion of hospitals, i.e., 64 hospitals, were in the DRS region; in financial performance, however, a majority of the hospitals (73 hospitals) were in the IRS region.

Our sample contained 43 hospitals that had fewer than 200 beds (small) and 47 hospitals that had 200 or more beds (large). In the operational performance stage, we saw a clear trend among the scale inefficient hospitals: a high proportion of both small hospitals (31 hospitals) and large hospitals (33 hospitals) were operating in the DRS region. In financial performance stage, however, among the scale inefficient hospitals, we observed that both small hospitals (34 hospitals) and large hospitals (39 hospitals) were operating in the IRS region.

Furthermore, our sample contained 37 rural hospitals and 53 urban hospitals. For operational performance, among the scale inefficient hospitals 23 rural hospitals and 41 urban hospitals operated in the DRS region. In the financial performance stage, among the scale inefficient hospitals a majority of the hospitals—29 rural and 44 urban—were in the IRS region.

In this study, RTS classification of the hospitals was based on their output-oriented VRS projections. According to Seiford and Zhu (1999), a different RTS classification may be obtained for a different orientation, since the input-oriented and the output-oriented VRS models can yield different projection points on the VRS frontier. Hence, we explored the robustness of the RTS classification under the input-oriented DEA method. Under the output-oriented DEA method, an IRS DMU must be termed as IRS by the input-oriented DEA method of Seiford and Zhu (1999). Therefore, we checked the CRS and DRS hospitals in the current study. Using Zhu and Shen (1995) input-oriented approach, we discovered that, on average, only four DRS hospitals in Stage 1 (operational performance) and two hospital in Stage 2 (financial performance) were termed as IRS hospitals for the input-oriented RTS method, which indicates that our RTS classification is robust and that, in general, the RTS classification in both stages is independent of the orientation of DEA model.

The findings from previous empirical research on the relationship between scale efficiency and hospital size are mixed (Leleu, Moises, & Valdmanis, 2012). Some studies found that larger hospitals operated better than the smaller ones, indicating the existence of economies of scale (Ferrier & Valdmanis, 2004; Goldstein, Ward, Leong, & Butler, 2002; Prior, 2006); while other studies concluded that smaller hospitals performed better than larger ones because the former were easier to manage (Huerta, Ford, Peterson, & Brigham, 2008; Oliveira & Bevan, 2008). Our results indicate that both small and large inefficient hospitals operate in the DRS region in operational performance and in the IRS region in financial performance.

From the economies of scale perspective, previous empirical research indicates that rural hospitals operate efficiently, albeit at a somewhat smaller bed size number (Finch & Christianson, 1981; Wang, Wan, Falk, & Goodwin, 2001). In both of these studies, the average bed size for rural hospitals was 113 and 107, respectively; whereas, in the current study the average bed size for rural hospitals was 171. Our results indicate that both rural and urban inefficient hospitals operate in the DRS region in operational performance and in the IRS region in financial performance. When the quality measures were excluded from the models, we found that an almost equal number of inefficient hospitals in the IRS and DRS regions in operational performance, and contrary to the previous results, a majority of inefficient hospitals were operating in the DRS region.

DISCUSSION AND CONCLUSIONS

This chapter has analyzed the operational and financial performance of 90 hospitals in Pennsylvania for 2013. The rising costs of operations and other challenges have put pressure on hospitals to improve their operational performance as well as financial performance. Hospitals may face a vicious cycle, wherein lower operational performance will lead to lower financial performance, which in turn may restrict access to capital and lead to lower investment in newer technology, and that then may affect operational performance. Previous DEA hospital efficiency studies have usually measured overall efficiency by using specific input and output variables. In contrast, this study has divided the hospital production process into two stages by transforming the inputs and outputs in each stage to reveal the efficiencies according to the production process and stage-wise role of inputs and outputs. Thus, we have added to the literature on the relationship between operational and financial performance by using a two-stage DEA model, which is a useful tool in assessing the efficacy of the hospital production process in terms of operational and financial performance. We also have added to the sparse literature that includes quality measures in hospital efficiency studies.

Using the two-stage CRS model, we found that close to 71% and 86% of the hospitals were inefficient in operations and financial performance, respectively. A single hospital, the Hospital University of Pennsylvania, was consistently efficient in both stages. We also found that hospitals could have produced about 13% more output in operational performance and about 54% more output in financial performance had they operated on the best frontier. We used the VRS model to compute scale efficiencies; we found that scale inefficiency is prevalent among the hospitals in Pennsylvania, with a majority of the hospitals exhibiting DRS in operational performance and IRS in financial performance. Diseconomies of scale in operational performance is in line with many previous studies (Becker & Sloan, 1985; Robinson, 1985; Robinson & Phibbs, 1990; Valdmanis 2010). We conjecture several reasons for this result: first, especially when quality measures are included, more registered nurse hours (labor intensive practices) are needed to deliver high quality care; second, as corroborated by relatively lower average occupancy rate of approximately 59% for the sample hospitals, there is an oversupply of beds relative to needs; finally, the average number of operating rooms at CRS is 12, while observed operating rooms is 14 (average). This indicates that operating rooms, which contain capital intensive, latest in surgical technology and sophisticated diagnostic equipment, are not optimally underutilized. As regards IRS in financial performance, in line with economic theory, an IRS frontier hospital would generally be in a more favorable position for expansion, compared to a hospital operating in a CRS or DRS region.

The limitations of this study broadly relate to methodology and sample selection. DEA requires that the decision-making units (i.e., hospitals) be homogeneous; however, it would be impossible to impose homogeneity on the hospitals in our sample, which vary in size, location, structure, and complexity of operations. A methodological limitation with the use of DEA is the specification error. The choice of inputs and outputs to the DEA model may impact the analyses of our results; moreover, DEA also is sensitive to the number of input and output variables. Therefore, the ability of our DEA model to discriminate among various employee and expense categories is limited. Finally, limiting the sample to hospitals in Pennsylvania may bring its own biases, which makes the generalization of our results to other states less obvious.

REFERENCES

Ali, A. I., & Seiford, L. M. (1990). Translation invariance in data envelopment analysis. *Operations Research Letters, 9*(6), 403–405.

Banker, R. D., Charnes, A., & Cooper, W. W. (1984). Some models for estimating technical and scale inefficiencies in data envelopment analysis. *Management Science, 30*(9), 1078–1092.

Banker, R. D., Conrad, R. F., & Strauss, R. P. (1986). A comparative application of data envelopment analysis and translog methods: An illustrative study of hospital production. *Management Science, 32*(1), 30–44.

Banker, R. D., & Thrall, R. M. (1992). Estimation of returns to scale using data envelopment analysis. *European Journal of Operational Research, 62*, 74–84.

Becker, E. R., & Sloan, F. A. (1985). Hospital ownership and performance. *Economic Inquiry, 23*(1), 21–36.

Burgess, J. F., & Wilson, P. W. (1996). Hospital ownership and technical efficiency. *Management Science, 42*(1), 110–123.

Charnes, A., Cooper, W. W., & Rhodes, E. (1978). Measuring the efficiency of decision-making units. *European Journal of Operational Research, 2*(6), 429–444.

Chilingerian, J. A., & Sherman, H. D. (2011). Healthcare applications: From hospitals to physicians, from productive efficiency to quality frontiers. In W. W. Cooper, L. M. Seiford, & J. Zhu (Eds.). *Handbook on data envelopment analysis.* New York, NY: Springer.

Chirikos, T. N., & Sear, A. M. (2000). Measuring hospital efficiency: A comparison of two approaches. *Health Services Research, 34*(6), 1389–1408.

Chowdhury, H., Zelenyuk, V., Laporte, A., & Wodchis, W. P. (2014). Analysis of productivity, efficiency and technological changes in hospital services in Ontario: How does case-mix matter? *International Journal of Production Economics, 150,* 74–82.

Clement, J. P., Valdmanis, V. G., Bazzoli, G. J., Zhao, M., & Chukmaitov, A. (2008). Is more better? An analysis of hospital outcomes and efficiency with a DEA model of output congestion. *Health Care Management Science, 11,* 67–77.

Coelli, T. J., & Perelman, S. (1999). A comparison of parametric and non-parametric distance functions: With applications to European railways. *European Journal of Operational Research, 117,* 326–339.

Cooper, W. W., Seiford, L. M., & Tone, K. (2000). *Data envelopment analysis.* Dordrecht, the Netherlands: Kluwer.

Elixhauser, A., & Andrews, R. M. (2010). Profile of inpatient operating room procedures in U.S. hospitals in 2007. *Archives of Surgery, 145*(12), 1201–1208.

Ferrier, G. D., & Trivitt, J. (2013). Incorporating quality into the measurement of hospital efficiency: A double DEA approach. *Journal of Productivity Analysis, 40*(3), 337–355.

Ferrier, G. D., & Valdmanis, V. G. (1996). Rural hospital performance and its correlates. *International Journal of Production Economics, 7*(1), 63–80.

Ferrier, G. D., & Valdmanis, (2004). Do mergers improve hospital productivity? *Journal of Operational Research Society, 55*(10), 1071–1080.

Finch, L. E., & Christianson, J. B., (1981). Rural hospital crisis: An analysis with policy implications. *Public Health Reports, 96,* 423–433.

Gaynor, M. S., Kleiner, S. A., & Vogt, W. B. (2014). Analysis of hospital production: An output index approach. *Journal of Applied Economics, 30*(3), 398–421.

Goldstein, S. M., Ward, P. T., Leong, G. K., & Butler, T. W. (2002). The effect of locations, strategy and operations technology on hospital performance. *Journal of Operations Management, 20,* 63–75.

Hollingsworth, B. (2003). Non-parametric and parametric applications measuring efficiency in health care. *Health Care Management Science, 6,* 203–218.

Hollingsworth, B. (2008). The measurement of efficiency and productivity of health care delivery. *Health Economics, 17*(10), 1107–1128.

Huerta, T. R., Ford, E. W., Peterson, L. T., & Brigham, H. H. (2008). Testing the hospital value proposition: An empirical analysis of efficiency and quality. *Health Care Management Review, 33,* 341–349.

Kohn, L. T., Corrigan, J. M., & Donaldson, M. S. (1999). *To err is human: Building a safer health system: Report of the Committee on Quality of Health Care in America, Institute of Medicine.* Washington, DC: National Academy Press

Leleu, H., Moises, J., & Valdmanis, V. G. (2012). Optimal productive size of hospital's intensive care units. *International Journal of Production Economics, 136,* 297–305.

McGlynn, E. R. (2008). *Identifying, categorizing, and evaluating health care efficiency measures: Final report.* Prepared by the Southern California Evidence-Based Practice Center, RAND Corporation, under Contract No. 282-00-0005-21. AHRQ Publication No. 08-0030.

Nayar, P., & Ozcan, Y. A. (2008). Data envelopment analysis comparison of hospital efficiency and quality. *Journal of Medical Systems, 32,* 193–199.

Nayar, P., Ozcan, Y. A., Yu, F., & Nguyen, A. T. (2013). Benchmarking urban acute care hospitals: Efficiency and quality perspectives. *Health Care Management Review, 38,* 137–145.

Newhouse, J. P. (1994). Frontier estimation: How useful a tool for health economics? *Journal of Health Economics, 13,* 317–322.

Nguyen, K. H., & Coelli, T. (2009). *Quantifying the effects of modelling choices on hospital efficiency measures: A meta-regression analysis: CEPA working papers series WP072009.* Brisbane, Australia: University of Queensland School of Economics.

Oliveira, M. D., & Bevan, G. (2008). Modelling hospitals costs to produce evidences that promote equity and efficiency. *European Journal of Operational Research, 185,* 933–947.

Ozcan, Y. A., & Bannick, R. R. (1994). Trends in Department of Defense hospital efficiency. *Journal of Medical Systems, 18,* 69–83.

Prior, D. (2006). Efficiency and total quality management in health care organizations: A dynamic frontier approach. *Annals Operations Research, 145,* 281–299.

Robinson, J. (1985). The impact of hospital market structure on patient volume, average length of stay, and the cost of care. *Journal of Health Economics, 4*(2), 333–536.

Robinson, J., & Phibbs, C. (1990). An evaluation of Medicaid selective contracting in California. *Journal of Health Economics, 8*(4), 437–456.

Seiford, L. M., & Zhu, J. (1999). Profitability and marketability of the top 55 U.S. commercial banks. *Management Science, 45*(9), 1270–1288.

Sultz, H. A., & Young, K. M. (2009). *Health care USA.* Burlington, MA: Jones & Bartlett.

Valdmanis, V. G. (2010). Measuring economies of scale at the city market level. *Journal of Health Care Finance, 37*(1), 78–90.

Valdmanis, V. G., Rosko, M. D., & Mutter, R. L. (2008). Hospital quality, efficiency, and input slack differentials. *Health Services Research, 43,* 1830–1848.

Wang, B. B., Wan, T. H., Falk, J. A., & Goodwin, D. (2001). Management strategies and financial performance in rural and urban hospitals. *Journal of Medical Systems, 25,* 241–255.

Weil, T. P. (2011). Privatization of hospitals: Meeting divergent interests. *Journal of Health Care Finance, 38*(2), 1–11.

Weiss A. J., & Elixhauser, A. (2014, March). *Trends in operating room procedures in U.S. hospitals, 2001–2011: HCUP statistical brief #171.* Retrieved from http://www. hcup-us.ahrq.gov/reports/statbriefs/sb171-Operating-Room-Procedure-Trends.pdf

Zhu, J., & Sen, Z. (1995). A discussion of testing DMUs' returns to scale. *European Journal of Operational Research, 81,* 590–596.

CHAPTER 5

DIGITAL DISRUPTION

How E-Commerce Is Changing the Grocery Game

Will Greerer
Nielsen Company

Gregory Smith, David Hyland, and Mark Frolick
Xavier University

ABSTRACT

The traditional grocery store business model is in a state of disruption, driven by the transition to selling groceries online via e-commerce. While online grocery sales are still minimal, they are expected to grow substantially as more retailers begin to compete in this space on convenience, access, and price. This article explores the primary methods of e-commerce product deployment in the grocery industry as well as the benefits and challenges posed by this new data-driven business model. To maximize its growth potential, the grocery e-commerce model may ultimately need to transition away from the existing store model where consumers gain access to products in traditional brick-and-mortar, high-dispersed environments to a new distribution system wholly reliant on information technology.

Contemporary Perspectives on Data Mining, Volume 3, pages 67–78
Copyright © 2018 by Information Age Publishing

The grocery industry stands at the brink of a potentially profound paradigm shift in the way it does business. Unlike many historical trends affecting the industry, this imminent shift is influenced not by trends in consumer taste preference or in the expansion of suburbia, but by food companies harnessing the power of information technology to distribute products in a way that is revolutionary to the industry, its structures, and those employed within it.

As a whole, U.S. retail e-commerce sales command $341.7 billion as of calendar 2015, up 14.6% from 2014 (U.S. Census Bureau, 2016). Total U.S. retail sales grew at only 1.4% in the same annual comparison. E-commerce sales made up 7.3% of total retail sales, and the pronounced growth rate demands attention.

However, despite the larger e-commerce channel's growth trend and phase of development, the grocery e-commerce subchannel is still in its infancy, estimated to represent only 1% of the total $600 billion grocery industry (Smith, 2015). While e-commerce makes up such a small share of the grocery business today, it is expected to develop at a compound annual growth rate (CAGR) of 21.1% from 2013 to 2018. By 2018, online grocery sales are expected to represent nearly $18 billion in the United States (Reagan, 2106).

Companies who invest now in the appropriate information technology systems, supply chains, distribution networks, and manufacturer partnerships are poised for success as consumers continue to gravitate toward purchasing groceries online. Those retailers who do not embrace the trend will run the risk of becoming obsolete in the long term, unable to capitalize on the shifting needs of consumers. Alternatively, retailers that do not have the economies of scale to adopt a large e-commerce presence will need to adapt to fill in gaps and provide different niche markets in order to compete and survive.

The purpose of this paper is to examine the driving forces behind e-commerce growth in the grocery industry, as well as discuss the benefits and limitations of the e-commerce grocery model.

DRIVING FORCES BEHIND E-COMMERCE GROWTH IN THE GROCERY INDUSTRY

Electronic commerce (e-commerce), was a term coined in the early 1990s and initially developed among consumers seeking out single-item purchases to meet specific, ad-hoc needs (Zhang, Zhu, & Ye, 2016). Key examples of products that were on the forefront of online shopping included consumer durable goods such as books and electronics.

There are a number of forces driving the shift from off-line and in-store sales to online sales in the grocery industry. Chief among these is the increasing availability of broadband, with internet penetration at home via any device standing at 88.5% of the population across the United States (Internet Live Stats, 2016). Additionally, many consumers have successfully and safely purchased consumer goods online for years, and have now acquired a level of comfort with this method. Because of this, they are willing to explore new purchase interactions, including those they make on a more ongoing basis, like grocery items (Mangiaracina, Marchet, Perotti, & Tumino, 2015).

Other key drivers facilitating the diffusion of e-commerce include enhanced consumer protections, embodied by a structured legal framework that addresses the unique nature of the online channel (Mangiaracina et al., 2015). The combination of a legal framework to protect against fraud and secure safe transactions, and the increased comfort of making purchases online creates a new level of trust and credibility to the online sales value proposition.

Another significant factor facilitating the advent of grocery e-commerce is the maturation of digital natives who incorporate technology into every aspect of their lives (Nielsen, 2015). Millennials, consumers between the ages of 18 and 34, embrace online shopping as a deeply ingrained, routine behavior and are open to purchasing groceries online. Consumer acceptance is expected to increase as Generation Z, the generation group following the Millennials, matures and begins making household purchases.

PRIMARY GROCERY E-COMMERCE MODELS

There are four primary models existing through today in which consumers purchase and gain access to groceries via e-commerce (Nielsen, 2015). Figure 5.1 shows the breakdown of acceptance for each model.

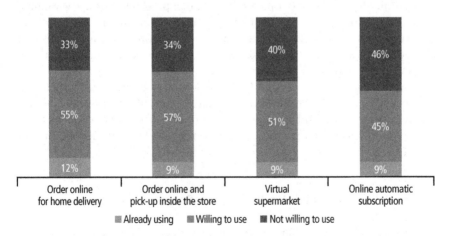

Figure 5.1 Percent using/willing to use grocery e-commerce options.

Order Online for Home Delivery

The most popular of the four models involves consumers ordering groceries online for home delivery. Twelve percent of consumers are already ordering groceries online for home delivery in the United States, and an additional 55% are willing to leverage this method (Nielsen, 2015). The key retailers operating within this model are primarily "pure play" retailers, i.e., those retailers who operate exclusively online and do not have physical store locations. Prime examples of the most successful retailers for this model include Amazon Fresh, Amazon Pantry, and Peapod (owned by Ahold USA).

Delivering a product direct to customers as opposed to having a customer pick up a product from a central location places an additional cost on the retailer. As such, the most successful deliver-to-home grocery retailers have required customers to pay a fee for the convenience. For example, according to Amazon's website, Amazon Fresh and Amazon Pantry are available only to those customers participating in the Amazon Prime service offered at $99/year (https://fresh.amazon.com/; http://www.amazon.com/gp/pantry/info). While this fee helps to offset shipping and delivery expenses, due to the low-margin nature of the grocery industry customers must also pay an additional fee for grocery home delivery from Amazon.

While each Amazon service delivers a strong value proposition to consumers, each is limited in its ability to fully replace its brick-and-mortar counterparts. While Amazon Fresh offers both food and nonfood household items, brand assortment is more limited and the service is only available in a handful of larger, predominantly West Coast urban markets (https://fresh.amazon.com/). Amazon Pantry, however, is available nationwide—excluding Alaska and Hawaii due to cost-prohibitive shipping costs—but offers a more limited assortment of only nonperishable products (http://www.amazon.com/gp/pantry/info). At this point, Amazon Fresh and Amazon Pantry are largely operating separately, but there is potential for a combined all-in-one service after the market has matured in geographic expansion and customer base.

Peapod, a subsidiary of Ahold USA, is available to customers for home delivery for a fee, and does not require an annual subscription. Peapod offers a range of food and nonfood households products. However, Peapod is only available in select markets, predominantly on the East Coast and Chicago (https://www.peapod.com/index.jhtml).

Order Online and Pick Up Inside the Store

The second most popular model within grocery e-commerce allows consumers to order groceries online for store pick-up. Nine percent of U.S.

consumers are already taking advantage of this unique operating model, and an additional 57% are willing to pick-up their online grocery order at the store (Nielsen, 2015). This model is employed primarily by those retailers who have historically competed in the grocery industry, i.e., brick-and-mortar retailers who operate with physical store locations. These stores offer an existing product inventory from which to distribute goods to customers, as well as available labor to pick-and-pack individualized grocery orders from existing store inventory.

Primarily, only larger mainstream grocery retailers have invested in making their goods available for customers to purchase online and pick up at the store to date. The Kroger Company, the nation's largest grocer, currently offers its ClickList service at 46 stores across the nation, with plans to offer ClickList at an additional 40 stores in the Houston and Dallas markets by the end of 2016 (Watkins, 2016). Harris Teeter, a regional mid-Atlantic supermarket chain owned by Kroger but operating separately, also offers the Click & Collect model through their ExpressLane service across 76 stores. Kroger's purchase of Harris Teeter has allowed the supermarket to expand its presence into markets where Kroger has not historically operated, as well as to acquire Harris Teeter's already developed e-commerce platform.

Virtual Supermarket

The third model is the virtual supermarket model. Virtual supermarkets exist as models through which consumers can gain access to groceries by purchasing online via a portal where shoppers can see the products they want on shelves that appear to be in a working supermarket. This model has garnered a lower level of adoption and acceptance across the United States than home delivery and in-store pick-up. Around 9% of consumers are already using virtual supermarkets in the United States with an additional 51% of consumers willing to leverage this method (Nielsen, 2015).

Virtual supermarkets attempt to meet customer needs based on the concept of making products available to hard-to-reach consumers who either will not or cannot make a regular trip to the grocery store. This model also resonates with shoppers who desire a robust shopping experience as similar as possible to the traditional physical, in-store environment. Up to 59% of consumers still rate their experience in physical stores as either "dramatically or somewhat better than their experience online" (Reporter, 2011).

While virtual supermarkets have seen success primarily in Asia and the United Kingdom in reaching busy urban commuters, there are fewer examples of companies operating with this business model effectively in the United States. One example that stands out in the virtual supermarket space is the regional northeastern/mid-Atlantic grocer ShopRite, which currently operates seven virtual supermarkets in Baltimore, Maryland, where one in four residents lives in a food desert (Babcock, 2015). The definition of a food desert is an area lacking fresh fruit, vegetables, and other helpful whole foods (Gallagher, 2011). In partnership with local organizations funded by grants, ShopRite opened virtual supermarkets near low-income senior housing facilities in 2015. This is also reportedly the first program in the nation where customers can pay for groceries online with EBT/food stamps.

Given the lower adoption rate of virtual supermarkets in the United States and the lack of a developed competitive set of retailers across local markets, virtual supermarkets may not develop as a lasting operating model or become engrained with shoppers like other methods of grocery e-commerce.

Online Automatic Subscription

The fourth and final model allows consumers to purchase groceries and food products via online automatic subscription services for delivery to their homes (Nielsen, 2015). The automatic nature of this model theoretically guarantees a more consistent revenue stream to businesses offering the service as customers must proactively cancel their orders. This gives grocery retailers a preview into expected demand on an on-going basis, allowing them to plan supply needs for their distribution facilities as well as partnerships with the manufacturers who make the goods available to the retailer for resale.

While the guaranteed revenue stream of online subscription services represents a benefit from a retailer's perspective, these companies typically do allow consumers the ability to cancel within a predetermined window of time prior to their order shipping. This safeguards functions to minimize customer concerns about being locked into a long-term service, and gains their initial participation with the assumption that once the customer signs on to the service, they will build their basket after experiencing the value proposition rather than cancel the service.

Amazon's Subscribe & Save is a premiere example of a national online automatic subscription service. Subscribe & Save enables customers to receive monthly shipments of food and nonfood household goods, placing consumers on autopilot, thus guaranteeing their loyalty and an ongoing revenue stream to Amazon (Rafiq, Fulford, & Lu, 2013). However, similar to Amazon Pantry, Amazon Subscribe & Save is currently limited only to nonperishable consumer goods without the appropriate framework or packaging capabilities in place to offer fresh goods that require freezing or refrigeration when shipped. Amazon's offering therefore does not have the ability to replace a shopper's entire grocery trip, although it poses a threat to a substantial portion of that regular trip. This segregation of grocery purchasing may create opportunities for smaller retailers without electronic economies of scale to create smaller store opportunities for consumers to purchase perishable and other items that are not purchased as part of a subscription based order.

Blue Apron, HelloFresh, and Plated are also popular online automatic subscription services that ship directly to consumers, though they are geared more to meal facilitation as opposed to pantry stocking. While this type of offering does pose a threat to the more traditional grocer's share of a customer's wallet, Blue Apron and others do not currently threaten to capture a shopper's entire weekly grocery trip, as do grocery e-commerce retailers offering a more comprehensive assortment.

BENEFITS OF GROCERY E-COMMERCE TO CONSUMERS AND BUSINESS

The four emerging models of grocery e-commerce offer new channels to reach existing customers, as well as attract a new set of customers. Shoppers now have the ability to purchase groceries at any time of day, from anywhere they want, and often from their preferred digital device, e.g., computer, phone, or tablet.

Enhanced Product Assortment and the Ability to Reach Niche Consumers

These new models of e-commerce offer enhanced product assortment to customers, as well as the ability to reach niche customer groups. As a prime example, there is a subset of the population with pronounced dietary needs that make it difficult or impossible to purchase products from a conventional grocery store (Benn, Webb, Chang, & Reidy, 2015). Those shoppers with severe instances of celiac disease may not be able to shop at their local supermarket whose planograms place gluten-free flour on the shelf below regular flour, presenting the risk of product contamination. Online grocery retailers can offer safe product guarantees, and also make small-scale and start-up brands available to customers nationwide when the brand may not yet be available in a customer's particular geographic market.

Some retailers are also taking advantage of third-party delivery facilitation now made available by such mobile-driven partners as Instacart (Bishop, 2015). Whole Foods has been partnering with Instacart since 2014, and recently expanded the partnership to double the number of Whole Foods stores that customers can have groceries delivered from (Springer, 2016). When retailers partner with data-rich third parties, they gain access to unprecedented amounts of customer information they did not have access to before. For a retailer like Whole Foods, which is considered a secondary shop by many customers and not their primary store, grocery e-commerce opens the door to significant new customer acquisition opportunities.

Grocery e-commerce also provides access and benefits to an aging population. The Age Gap survey indicates that 57% of seniors are concerned about losing physical agility as they age and find making in-store grocery shopping an increasingly challenging task (Nielsen, 2014). Compared to other global markets, North America ranks number one among older consumers in terms of the availability of online shopping delivery options. When marketing groceries to older consumers online, this population has a unique set of needs characterized by greater concern about information security and fraud, as well as more frustration about the level of product detail made available online in an easy-to-read format (Leppel & McCloskey, 2011). Online grocers will need to pay careful attention to meeting the needs of older populations in their online site and mobile application interfaces, while not alienating younger customers by making the platforms too simplistic.

Building Loyalty and Basket Size Online

The various grocery e-commerce models embody characteristics that will build loyalty and basket size among customers with the right implementation. Many traditional brick-and-mortar retailers who now offer the Click & Collect model for pick up in the store provide the ability for customers to save their grocery lists to use on future trips. Once the list is built, customers do not need to spend the time physically walking aisles or digitally re-creating shopping lists. The information is already there electronically and customers can easily add to or remove items. Such ease-of-use can translate into higher loyalty to a retailer, in effect taking the shopper out of the marketplace.

When customers have grocery e-commerce options in their local market, many prefer to purchase groceries online from their preferred offline store (Melis, Campo, Breugelmans, & Lamey, 2015). Kroger, Giant, Stop & Shop, and Whole Foods are taking advantage of their strong equity to enter the game early and gradually expand their market reach. While a barrier for some customers to online grocery shopping is a concern about bruised products or the inability to personally select their own meat and produce, some retailers have actually found that online shopping has created more personal relationships with shoppers. It is not uncommon for customers to leave comments in the "special notes" sections of their orders requesting that they only want the product if Sam or Sally is hand picking the items.

Labor Cost and Real Estate Savings

Brick-and-mortar retailers can also save on labor and real estate costs when they move to a model more focused around online shopping. While there is substantial cost in adding pick-and-pack duties to in-store employees' current responsibilities, there may be a reduced need for customer-facing employees in the future and an increased need for behind-the-scenes, potentially lower paid warehouse workers (Reagan, 2016). Walmart is already experimenting with this method in northwest Arkansas at an exclusively Click & Collect location that has no in-store area for customers to visit; customers arrive purely for pick-up (Springer, 2014).

Some markets have also seen an inverse relationship between commercial real estate and the rise of e-commerce. As e-commerce expands, and the location and operating hour barriers of traditional, physical commerce are removed, commercial property sales have slowed while vacancies have increased. The reduced need to build, maintain, and operate large-box retail stores offers the potential to provide large-scale, real-estate cost savings (Zhang, Zu, & Ye, 2016).

CHALLENGES FACING GROCERY E-COMMERCE

Limitations of Existing IT Systems

A key challenge retailers face as they expand online grocery offerings is that many of the brick-and-mortar legacy systems do not integrate with the different priorities of online models (Reagan, 2016). Traditional brick-and-mortar inventory systems must be re-operationalized from an information technology perspective, as many do not account for online transactions on inventory stock levels in the brick-and-mortar, in-store system (Anderson, 2016). Often, employees who are picking and packing online customer orders are competing with in-store customers for the same products on the shelf, resulting in out-of-stock items and less satisfied online customers who now have incomplete orders.

Many retailers also currently implement store-specific and market-specific pricing strategies at their brick-and-mortar stores. Currently, it is now common practice for Click & Collect retailers to offer items online at the same price as in-store, but this is contrastingly different than pure-play retailers like Amazon, who offer one consistent price via Subscribe & Save, Amazon Pantry, and other services. Retailers will need to think through local market pricing dynamics carefully to optimize profits as an increasingly larger portion of their business comes from online sales. Similar to inventory management systems, this new pricing strategy will require significant alterations to existing information technology, or the creation of entirely new IT software and systems.

Packaging Costs and Environmental Considerations

The supply chain networks of grocery e-commerce players will need to continue to evolve as demand increases for online grocery products. Warehousing, transportation planning and management, and packaging each represent significant cost savings or expenses that must be carefully considered in a retailer's information technology systems and distribution networks (Mangiaracina et al., 2015).

Grocery e-commerce retailers may need to consider establishing minimum basket size requirements to combat inefficient deliveries of single-item or small orders whose delivery costs may exceed the profit coming from the order. The need for additional individualized packaging to preserve perishable products for home delivery is also a contributor to greenhouse gas emissions, and generates unnecessary waste compared to bulk shipment methods at brick-and-mortar stores. Click & Collect models do not impose the same packaging and delivery-to-home environmental costs, as the cost of delivery is placed on the customer who arrives in person to pick up the order.

CONCLUSION

While the grocery industry is still in the infancy stage of e-commerce development, many companies are implementing models that are profoundly shifting the ways retailers conduct business with consumers. Consumers are demanding increased levels of convenience and quality as they leverage the power of digital devices to meet their everyday needs. Grocers must rise to the challenge or risk becoming obsolete. Retailers will need to cater to the unique needs of individual consumer groups and capitalize on the digital disruption created by the new e-commerce.

One challenge that has briefly been discussed in this chapter, and an area for ongoing research, is the utilization of the data being created both in traditional store experiences via checkout and scanning devices, and through e-commerce. The electronic interaction with customers creates a plethora of data for businesses to use. Data mining the increasingly vast amounts of customer data afforded by electronic commerce is creating opportunities for the improvement of pricing, distribution, and product offerings (Bishop, 2015).

This new information technology will increasingly shift the ways of doing business, altering the need for physical stores, which may not be able to compete as effectively with online-only businesses that have lower overhead costs. Physical grocery stores may disappear as has occurred in the music, video, book, and electronics industries. The question remains which model of grocery e-commerce will win out, or whether there will be a mix of offerings available to meet the needs of varying segments across urban and rural markets. There is one certainty: innovation in information technology is changing the grocery industry and will continue to do so.

REFERENCES

Anderson, K. (2016, April 8). *Click-and-collect continues to evolve, but where is it headed?* Retrieved April 10, 2016, from http://supermarketnews.com/blog/click-and-collect-continues-evolve-where-it-headed

Babcock, S. (2015, December 29). *Baltimore now has 7 virtual supermarket locations: Technically Baltimore.* Retrieved April 9, 2016, from http://technical.ly/baltimore/2015/12/29/baltimore-now-7-virtual-supermarket-locations/

Benn, Y., Webb, T. L., Chang, B. I., & Reidy, J. (2015). What information do consumers consider, and how do they look for it, when shopping for groceries online? *Appetite, 89,* 265–273. doi:10.1016/j.appet.2015.01.025

Bishop, B. (2015, July 7). *Pondering Instacart's power position.* Retrieved April 10, 2016, from http://supermarketnews.com/online-retail/pondering-instacarts-power-position

Gallagher, M. (2011). USDA defines food deserts. *Nutrition Digest, 38*(2). Retrieved September 12, 2016, from http://americannutritionassociation.org/newsletter/usda-defines-food-deserts

Internet Live Stats. (2016). (n.d.). *Internet users by country.* Retrieved April 9, 2016, from http://www.internetlivestats.com/internet-users-by-country/

Leppel, K., & McCloskey, D. W. (2011). A cross-generational examination of electronic commerce adoption. *Journal of Consumer Marketing, 28*(4), 261–268. doi:10.1108/07363761111143150

Mangiaracina, R., Marchet, G., Perotti, S., & Tumino, A. (2015). A review of the environmental implications of B2C e-commerce: A logistics perspective. *International Journal of Physical Distribution and Logistics Management, 45*(6), 565–591. doi:10.1108/IJPDLM-06-2014-0133

Melis, K., Campo, K., Breugelmans, E., & Lamey, L. (2015). The impact of the multichannel retail mix on online store choice: Does online experience matter? *Journal of Retailing, 91*(2), 272–288. doi:10.1016/j.jretai.2014.12.004

Nielson. (2014, February 25). *The age gap.* Retrieved from http://www.nielsen.com/us/en/insights/reports/2014/the-age-gap.html

Nielsen. (2015, April 29). *The future of grocery: E-commerce, digital technology, and changing shopping preferences around the world.* Retrieved from http://www.nielsen.com/us/en/insights/reports/2015/the-future-of-grocery.html

Rafiq, M., Fulford, H., & Lu, X. (2013). Building customer loyalty in online retailing: The role of relationship quality. *Journal of Marketing Management, 29*(3/4), 494–517. doi:10.1080/0267257X.2012.737356

Reagan, C. (2016, January 13). *Like it or not, 'click and collect' is here to stay.* Retrieved April 10, 2016, from http://www.cnbc.com/2016/01/13/like-it-or-not-click-and-collect-is-here-to-stay.html

Reporter, D. M. (2011, August 1). *Express delivery: How you can buy your groceries from a virtual supermarket ... on a train platform.* Retrieved April 10, 2016, from http://www.dailymail.co.uk/sciencetech/article-2021064/How-buy-groceries-virtual-supermarket—train-platform.html

Smith, C. (2015, June 18). *Here's why groceries are the biggest untapped e-commerce opportunity.* Retrieved April 9, 2016, from http://www.businessinsider.com/startups-ecommerce-giants-create-winners-losers-grocery-markets-2015-6

Springer, J. (2014, September 29). *Gallery: Walmart opens Click-and-Collect facility.* Retrieved April 10, 2016, from http://supermarketnews.com/online-retail/gallery-walmart-opens-click-and-collect-facility#slide-4-field_images-491801

Springer, J. (2016, March 10). *Whole Foods, Instacart to expand partnership.* Retrieved April 9, 2016, from http://supermarketnews.com/online-retail/whole-foods-instacart-expand-partnership

U.S. Census Bureau. (2016). *Quarterly retail e-commerce sales, 4th quarter 2015.* Retrieved from https://www.census.gov/retail/index.html

Watkins, S. (2016, March 31). *Kroger expands online ordering to two major markets.* Retrieved April 9, 2016, from http://www.bizjournals.com/cincinnati/news/2016/03/31/kroger-expands-online-ordering-to-two-major.html

Zhang, D., Zhu, P., & Ye, Y. (2016). The effects of e-commerce on the demand for commercial real estate. *Cities, 51,* 106–120. doi:10.1016/j.cities.2015.11.012

CHAPTER 6

THE HAZARDS OF SUBGROUP ANALYSIS IN RANDOMIZED BUSINESS EXPERIMENTS AND HOW TO AVOID THEM

B. D. McCullough
Drexel University

ABSTRACT

Experiments are ever more widely used in business. Frequently the experimental units are represented in databases with available covariates, raising the opportunity for subgroup analysis. There are two types of subgroups analyses: hypothesis generation and hypothesis testing. The former is very easy to do, but the latter is difficult. We offer an example of subgroup analysis that shows the pitfalls, and gives rules for avoiding the pitfalls. We also provide a dataset that can be used for classroom exercises.

The use of subgroups analysis in the context of randomized experiments has a long history in medical research, but is notably absent from the business research literature. In part, this is due to the fact that the use of experimental design also has a long history in medical research, but experiments

Contemporary Perspectives on Data Mining, Volume 3, pages 79–91
Copyright © 2018 by Information Age Publishing

are a relatively recent addition to the business research methodology. We could find practically no references to subgroup analysis in the business literature, despite its widespread use in the business world. For example, the problem of targeting a marketing campaign can be cast as finding a population subgroup that would be interested in purchasing a particular item. One of the few references we could find was in a *Harvard Business Review* article by Anderson and Simester (2011): "A Step-by-Step Guide to Smart Business Experiments." The authors advise conducting subgroup analyses after the experiment has been conducted. This is good advice, but it is easier said than done. Looking at subgroups is very easy; actually determining whether a subgroup-specific effect exists is difficult. Here we offer much-needed advice on how to conduct a subgroup analysis properly. We also offer a dataset and a set of exercises that can be used in the classroom to give students practice in subgroup analysis.

It is worthwhile to quote Anderson and Simester's advice on this, the fourth of their seven points:

4. When the results come in, slice the data.

When customers are randomly assigned to treatment and control groups, and there are many customers in each group, then you may effectively have multiple experiments to analyze. For example, if your sample includes both men and women, you can evaluate the outcome with men and women separately. Most actions affect some customers more than others. So when the data arrive, look for subgroups within your control and treatment groups. If you examine only aggregate data, you may incorrectly conclude that there no effects on any customers.

The characteristics that you use to group customers, such as gender or historical purchasing patterns, must be independent of the action itself. For example, if you want to analyze how a store opening affects catalog demand, you cannot simply compare customers who made a purchase at the store with customers who did not. The results will reflect existing customer differences rather than the impact of opening the store. Consider instead comparing purchases by customers who live close to the new store versus customers who live far away. As long as the two groups are roughly equivalent, the differences in their behavior can be attributed to the store opening. (Anderson & Simester, 2011)

Several important questions come to mind: How to choose which subgroups to investigate? How many subgroups to investigate? How to separate real effects from Type I errors? How to avoid Type II errors? and more. We shall illustrate the importance of these points by conducting a typical subgroup analysis that pays no attention to these important details.

First, however, we remark that poorly executed subgroup analyses are common. The medical literature is filled with articles describing such analyses, and also with articles debunking the conclusions thereof. The medical literature has many articles with entertaining titles such as "How to Guarantee Finding a Statistically Significant Difference: The Use and Abuse of Subgroup Analyses" (Fayers & King, 2009), "Beware of Subgroup Analysis" (Mitsnefes, Khoury, & Devarajan, 2008), "Misleading Subgroup Analyses in GISSI" (Peto, 1990), and "The Problem of Subgroup Analyses: An Example from a Trial on Ruptured Intracranial Aneurysms" (Nagarra, Raymond, Guilbert, & Altman, 2011). In one famous case, the editor of a journal insisted that the authors of an experimental article include a subgroup analysis. The authors knew that such an analysis would be unreliable (i.e., due to deficient sample size) and demurred. The editor then demanded that such an analysis be included or he wouldn't publish the paper. To satisfy the editor and yet not mislead readers, the authors used astrological signs as a subgroup to show that aspirin was an ineffective treatment for patients whose sign was Libra or Gemini. The story is recounted by one of the authors of the original article, Peto (2005).

To keep our presentation generic, we shall neither identify the experiment conducted nor the covariates available. Y is the response variable, X is a dummy variable indicating 0 for control and 1 for treatment, so a two-sample t-test of Y on X yields the results of the experiment. $Z1, Z2, \ldots Z10$ are binary covariates arranged in order of increasing proportion and $Z11$–$Z12$ are continuous covariates. The sample size is $n = 1000$. Summary statistics on the variables are presented in Table 6.1, binary covariates on the left and continuous covariates on the right. A fuller exploratory data analysis, the details of which are omitted, would include histograms, boxplots, scatterplots, etc. For example, X might be two different prices offered to customers, Y would measure how much was purchased in response to the

TABLE 6.1 Summary Statistics on Variables						
Variable	Mean	Variable	Mean	St. Dev.	Min	Max
X	0.50	Y	9.95	4.14	−2.03	25.24
Z1	0.06	Z11	0.49	0.29	0	1
Z2	0.12	Z12	0.60	0.20	0.05	0.99
Z3	0.15	Z13	1.03	1.06	0.00	7.77
Z4	0.22	Z14	3.09	3.97	−9.75	15.45
Z5	0.24	Z15	0.88	0.44	0.04	2.80
Z6	0.30	Z16	3.98	1.83	−7.68	9.55
Z7	0.34	Z17	1.52	1.25	0.02	7.64
Z8	0.42	Z18	1.23	0.76	0.19	6.65
Z9	0.44	Z19	3.52	0.87	2.01	4.49
Z10	0.49	Z20	4.98	2.23	−2.60	12.03

offer, Z1–Z10 might be various demographic variables, such as distance traveled to work, median neighborhood income, number of persons in the household, etc., while Z11–Z20 might indicate whether the customer has made prior purchases from any of 10 different categories.

The usual two-sample test of means applied to Y and X produces a 95% confidence interval (CI) of (–0.27, 0.76) for the average treatment effect with a p-value of 0.343. Since the CI covers the origin, the average treatment effect is zero for the population. Following Anderson and Simester's advice, we test subgroups to see whether the treatment might have an effect in a subgroup. With respect to the binary covariate Z1 there are two obvious subgroups, those observations for which $Z1 = 0$ and those for which $Z1 = 1$; similarly for the remaining nine binary covariates. Results for testing these subgroups are presented in Table 6.2.

At the 5% level, we find two subgroups with significant treatment effects: $Z7 = 0$ and $Z4 = 1$. At the 10% level there are three additional subgroups with significant treatment effects: $Z3 = 0$, $Z1 = 1$ and $Z3 = 1$.

Of course, "drilling down" to find subgroups of subgroups is a commonly used exploratory technique. For example, Married might be a group, and Married With Children is a subgroup that has its own subgroups—e.g., Married With Children, Living in the Suburbs, as opposed to Married, No Children, Living in the City. The purchasing patterns of these subgroups is distinctly different, and the latter two subgroups are formed as the intersection of three categories, e.g., those who are married, those who have no children, and those who live in the city. Experian has broken American consumers into 19 groups, and each of these is broken down further. The

TABLE 6.2	Results for Testing Subgroups				
Subgroup	95% CI for Subgroup Treatment Effect	p-value	Subgroup	95% CI for Subgroup Treatment Effect	p-value
Z1 = 0	(–0.13, 0.92)	0.139	Z1 = 1	(–4.69, 0.20)	0.071
Z2 = 0	(–0.16, 0.95)	0.159	Z2 = 1	(–2.27, 0.56)	0.233
Z3 = 0	(–0.03, 1.08)	0.063	Z3 = 1	(–2.54, 0.15)	0.082
Z4 = 0	(–0.59, 0.56)	0.949	Z4 = 1	(0.11, 2.39)	0.032*
Z5 = 0	(–0.52, 0.66)	0.817	Z5 = 1	(–0.27, 1.81)	0.145
Z6 = 0	(–0.20, 0.98)	0.197	Z6 = 1	(–1.11, 0.93)	0.869
Z7 = 0	(0.02, 12.8)	0.043*	Z7 = 1	(–1.46, 0.36)	0.232
Z8 = 0	(–0.51, 0.84)	0.627	Z8 = 1	(–0.41, 1.18)	0.344
Z9 = 0	(–0.60, 0.77)	0.817	Z9 = 1	(–0.32, 1.24)	0.245
Z10 = 0	(–0.62, 0.81)	0.786	Z10 = 1	(–0.34, 1.14)	0.292

* Denotes significant treatment effect at the 5% level.

Suburban Style group consists of Sports Utility Families, Settled in Suburbia, Cul de Sac Diversity and Suburban Attainment subgroups. Let us drill down a bit into our dataset.

First let us consider intersections of $Z1$ with other binary variables, i.e., $Z1$ is the primary variable. If we consider $Z1$ intersecting with $Z2$, we can form four groups: $Z1 = 0$ & $Z2 = 0$; $Z1 = 0$ & $Z2 = 1$; $Z1 = 1$ & $Z2 = 0$; $Z1 = 1$ & $Z2 = 1$. Similarly, $Z1$ can intersect with $Z3, Z4, \ldots Z10$. Table 6.3 presents the results of such an analysis only for the $Z1$ intersection subgroups, of which there are four in each of the nine rows. Out of the 36, there are six subgroups with significant treatment effects at the 5% level, denoted with an asterisk next to the p-value.

Considering intersections with $Z2$ as the primary variable, there are only eight rows for a total of 32 intersections; since $Z2$ intersected with $Z1$ is the same as $Z1$ intersected with $Z2$, and we already did the latter. Similarly, for $Z3$ as the primary, there are only seven rows for a total of 28 intersections. Table 6.4 shows the number of intersections and the number of subgroups with significant treatment effects at the 5% level. There is no row for $Z10$ because all $Z10$ intersections have been accounted for in previous rows. Table 6.4 shows that of 180 intersections tested, there were 15 significant effects at the 5% level.

Matters get more complicated when we examine the continuous covariates. We have to cut the continuous variable into groups to form categorical variables. A common approach for doing this is to examine the shapes of the distributions and pick a point to create a pair of binary variables representing "high" and "low" values, or pick two points to obtain "low," "medium," and "high" values. Consider, for example, the histogram with density overlaid of variable $Z12$ shown in Figure 6.1. Low, medium, and high would be reasonable, and so we chose cutpoints 0.25 and 0.75. We could have chosen 0.2 and 0.8, or 0.1 and 0.9, but we didn't. If 0.25/0.75 doesn't work, we aren't going to try 0.2/0.8 because we're not data dredging. Similarly, for $Z14$ we chose −7/+12. $Z18$ appears to have two regions, the bulk of the data and a long tail, so we chose 2.5; again, we could have chosen 2.25 or 2.75, but we didn't. For $Z20$ we choose 3/7.

Table 6.5 shows the cutpoints we chose and significant results. If there is one cutpoint, then H for high or L for low might be significant; if two cutpoints, there will also be an M for middle. As it turned out, all the subgroups with significant treatment effects were in the H subgroup. Table 6.5 shows that we have uncovered three subgroups with significant treatment effects at the 5% level: $Z14 > 12$; $Z18 > 2.5$; and $Z20 > 7$. An additional two subgroups with significant treatment effects at the 10% level are: $Z12 > 0.75$ and $Z17 > 1.75$.

We have not considered intersections between the binary and continuous covariates, nor have we considered three-way intersections. But we

TABLE 6.3 Results of Analysis for Z1 Intersection Subgroups

Group	p-value	Group	p-value	Group	p-value	Group	p-value
$Z1 = 0$ & $Z2 = 0$	0.060*	$Z1 = 0$ & $Z2 = 1$	0.364	$Z1 = 1$ & $Z2 = 0$	0.140	$Z1 = 1$ & $Z2 = 1$	0.276
$Z1 = 0$ & $Z3 = 0$	0.173	$Z1 = 0$ & $Z3 = 1$	0.021*	$Z1 = 1$ & $Z3 = 0$	0.230	$Z1 = 1$ & $Z3 = 1$	0.021*
$Z1 = 0$ & $Z4 = 0$	0.500	$Z1 = 0$ & $Z4 = 1$	0.054	$Z1 = 1$ & $Z4 = 0$	0.007*	$Z1 = 1$ & $Z4 = 1$	0.291
$Z1 = 0$ & $Z5 = 0$	0.431	$Z1 = 0$ & $Z5 = 1$	0.112	$Z1 = 1$ & $Z5 = 0$	0.102	$Z1 = 1$ & $Z5 = 1$	0.837
$Z1 = 0$ & $Z6 = 0$	0.099	$Z1 = 0$ & $Z6 = 1$	0.799	$Z1 = 1$ & $Z6 = 0$	0.329	$Z1 = 1$ & $Z6 = 1$	0.080
$Z1 = 0$ & $Z7 = 0$	0.009*	$Z1 = 0$ & $Z7 = 1$	0.289	$Z1 = 1$ & $Z7 = 0$	0.075	$Z1 = 1$ & $Z7 = 1$	0.364
$Z1 = 0$ & $Z8 = 0$	0.472	$Z1 = 0$ & $Z8 = 1$	0.134	$Z1 = 1$ & $Z8 = 0$	0.378	$Z1 = 1$ & $Z8 = 1$	0.031*
$Z1 = 0$ & $Z9 = 0$	0.500	$Z1 = 0$ & $Z9 = 1$	0.146	$Z1 = 1$ & $Z9 = 0$	0.132	$Z1 = 1$ & $Z9 = 1$	0.322
$Z1 = 0$ & $Z10 = 0$	0.582	$Z1 = 0$ & $Z10 = 1$	0.122	$Z1 = 1$ & $Z10 = 0$	0.222	$Z1 = 1$ & $Z10 = 1$	0.136

* Denotes significant treatment effects at the 5% level.

TABLE 6.4 Number of Intersections and Subgroups With Significant Treatment Effects

Primary variable	# of intersection subgroups	# of subgroups with significant treatment effects
Z1	36	6
Z2	32	3
Z3	28	3
Z4	24	0
Z5	20	1
Z6	16	0
Z7	12	2
Z8	8	0
Z9	4	0

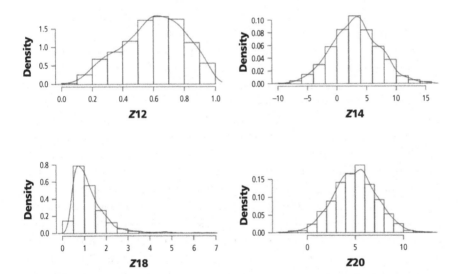

Figure 6.1 Histogram with density overlaid of variable Z12.

could do all of these things. The scope for creating subgroups increases dramatically with the number of covariates. As it stands, we have performed a standard subgroup analysis at the 5% level without excessive data dredging and found two binary subgroups without intersections and five continuous subgroups without intersections. Using intersections on the binary data, we found 15 subgroups with significant treatment effects. Overall, we have found 22 significant subgroup effects.

Variable	Cutpoint(s)	Significant L/M/H?	95% CI for Treatment Effect	p-value
Z11	0.2/0.8			
Z12	0.25/0.75	H	(−0.13, 1.99)	0.084
Z13	0.25			
Z14	−7/12	H	(1.29, 10.30)	0.016
Z15	0.25/1.75			
Z16	0/8			
Z17	1.75	H	(−0.08, 1.61)	0.077
Z18	2.5	H	(−4.00, −0.17)	0.033
Z19	2.5/4.5			
Z20	3/7	H	(0.006, 2.51)	0.049

TABLE 6.5 Cutpoints and Significant Results

The astute reader will wonder: How many of the 22 significant results are false positives (Type I errors)? We conducted 20 tests on the binary variables, 180 tests on the binary intersections, and 27 on the continuous variables for a total of 229 tests. At the 5% level, we would expect 11.45 false positives. We found almost twice as many significant results as one would expect if there were no effects. Surely we found some real subgroups and not all of our significant results are spurious. But which ones? Despite our protestations to the contrary, we have engaged in some serious data dredging, and we have no way to know which significant results might indicate real subgroup effects and which are purely spurious. This is the Achilles heel of the shotgun approach to subgroup analysis. What have we found with all our slicing and dicing? Nothing. We have found nothing that is actionable. The only way to separate the real from the spurious is to conduct 22 experiments on our 22 new hypotheses. What we have done is subgroup analysis for hypothesis generation, not subgroup analysis for hypothesis testing.

Subgroup analysis is plagued by both Type I and Type II errors. The former were discussed in the previous paragraph. The latter arise because, absent specific planning by the analyst, subgroups may not have a large enough sample to detect effects that are really there, i.e., the tests are underpowered. In fact, if the main effect is powered properly, then most of the subgroups are destined to be underpowered. Both these problems of excess Type I and excess Type II errors can exist simultaneously. Type I errors are due to multiple hypothesis testing, and Type II errors are due to deficient sample size. Since they have different sources, they cannot be traded off and must be resolved separately. If you plan to do subgroup analysis for hypothesis testing, conduct a power analysis *before* the experiment to make sure that the subgroups of interest have enough observations to detect an effect.

The medical literature has wrestled with the problem of subgroup analysis for many years, and has developed a sensible approach to conducting subgroup analyses so that the results of hypothesis tests can be trusted (more or less). There are many variations on this theme, the original being Oxman and Guyatt (1992); more recent refinements are Rothwell (2005) and Burke, Sussman, Kent, and Hayward, (2015). Here we adapt their guidelines by dropping rules that only apply to medical research. We propose five rules in no particular order:

1. The subgroups hypotheses must be defined before the experiment is conducted. This prevents ex-post data dredging.
2. The subgroups must be justified. There must be some justification for the hypothesis, be it empirical (prior observational data have suggested the effect might exist) or not (this subgroup analysis is a first, tentative test of some proposed theory).
3. The subgroup hypotheses must be few in number to prevent the multiple comparisons problem. If more than a few hypotheses are tested, we run the very real risk of having a couple significant results, but know that at least one is a false positive. In this situation we have learned nothing by conducting the subgroup experiments, because we have to run more experiments to separate fact from fiction.
4. Each subgroup hypothesis test must be sufficiently powered, i.e., the subgroup should have enough observations to reliably detect a true effect. This requires the researcher to specify an effect size and perform a power analysis.
5. Is the effect size important? In the business setting is the magnitude worth worrying about? An experiment that produces a 3-cent increase on a product that sells for tens of dollars probably isn't worth implementing. This is why we focus on CIs not on p-values; p-values do not inform us about the magnitude of the effect. If a cost/benefit analysis justifies the expense, then conduct another experiment before implementing it on a large scale. On the other hand, if the subgroup effect—if it really exists—is small and won't add much to the bottom line, then there is no point in pursuing it.

One consequence of not following these rules when performing subgroup analysis is that it is very easy for the poorly trained or even unscrupulous analyst to produce "statistically significant" treatments for some subgroups. When the previously mentioned rules are followed, the analyst can have some degree of certainty regarding the results of a subgroup analysis. Figure 6.2 illustrates the importance of Rule 3. For $\alpha = 0.05$, when the number

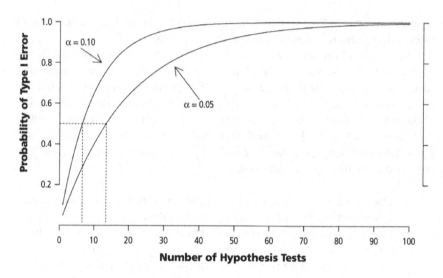

Figure 6.2 Importance of subgroup hypotheses being few in number.

of hypothesis tests $n = 13.51$, the overall probability of a Type I error is 50%. For $\alpha = 0.10$, when $n = 6.58$ the overall probability of a Type I error is 50%. Testing just seven hypotheses, there's a 50% chance you'll be in the situation where you don't know whether a significant result is real or spurious. To avoid this, the number of hypotheses tested must be small, by this we mean one or two (Varadhan & Seeger, 2013) and certainly fewer than six (Sun et al., 2012). If the number of hypotheses is small, then the expected number of significant results due to chance will be less than one, and we can be somewhat confident that any significant results are real. On the other hand, once the expected number of significant results due to chance exceeds one, we cannot be sure than a particular significant result is not spurious. In our example, we were able to generate over 100 hypotheses with little difficulty, and we didn't even consider three-way intersections. We were doomed to failure if the goal of the exercise was subgroup analysis for hypothesis testing. On the other hand, if our goal was subgroup analysis for hypothesis generation, we didn't do too badly.

In fact, all the significant results we found were spurious. We know this because all the variables were created by calls to a random number generator. Nonetheless, because we were data dredging, we were able to uncover many "statistically significant" results, spurious though each of them was. It would have been an easy matter to find more significant results for the continuous covariates. It is trivially easy to find significant cutpoints for the continuous covariates. Let Z be the covariate; form the matrix with columns

TABLE 6.6 Cutpoints and *p*-Values Discovered by Algorithm		
Variable	Cutpoint	*p*-value
Z11	0.039	0.073
Z12	0.574	0.014
Z13	0.49	0.048
Z14	10.038	0.041
Z15	0.891	0.075
Z16	3.518	0.069
Z17	2.911	0.004
Z18	3.453	0.003
Z19	4.727	0.015
Z20	6.442	0.020

Z, Y, and X; and sort the rows of the matrix according to Z. Be sure that whatever cutpoint you choose leaves enough observations so that a valid statistical test can be carried out. For example, choosing cutpoint $= \min(Z)$ would fail to satisfy this requirement. Since there are 1,000 observations, we started at the 50th ordered value of Z and continued ascending to the 950th ordered value, testing each as a cutpoint, and choosing the cutpoint that produced the smallest p-value. Accordingly, Table 6.6 gives the cutpoints and *p*-values discovered by this algorithm. Seven of the 10 have p-values less than 0.05, and none of these covariates has anything to do with the experimental variables.

In our teaching, we have found that it is one thing to tell students about the dangers of subgroup analysis, and it is something else altogether when the students discover this for themselves. We like to ask the students to find some significant subgroups. After doing this, we ask them to compute the expected number of Type I errors. Then we ask them which of their significant results are "real" and which are due to Type I errors. It begins to dawn on them that they can't tell one from the other, and it really brings home the point that they have been data dredging (usually without actually realizing it).

This forces students to realize that they have to decide whether they want to test hypotheses or generate hypotheses before they begin doing subgroup analysis. While these two goals are very different, the unskilled analyst often thinks he's performing the former when he's actually doing the latter.

The dataset we have used in this chapter lends itself to a variety of useful exercises. We produced the dataset using Microsoft R Open v3.2.4, the code follows:

```
set.seed(1)
mysampsize <- 1000
Y = rnorm(mysampsize,10,4)
# X must be exactly half zeroes and half ones
Z1 <- rep(0,mysampsize/2)
Z2 <- rep(1,mysampsize/2)
X <- c(Z1,Z2)
X = sample(X,mysampsize,replace=FALSE)
Z1 <- rbinom(mysampsize,1,0.05)
Z2 <- rbinom(mysampsize,1,0.10)
Z3 <- rbinom(mysampsize,1,0.15)
Z4 <- rbinom(mysampsize,1,0.20)
Z5 <- rbinom(mysampsize,1,0.25)
Z6 <- rbinom(mysampsize,1,0.30)
Z7 <- rbinom(mysampsize,1,0.35)
Z8 <- rbinom(mysampsize,1,0.40)
Z9 <- rbinom(mysampsize,1,0.45)
Z10 <- rbinom(mysampsize,1,0.50)
Z11 <- runif(mysampsize)
Z12 <- rbeta(mysampsize,3,2)
Z13 <- rexp(mysampsize,1)
Z14 <- rnorm(mysampsize,3,4)
Z15 <- rweibull(mysampsize,2)
Z16 <- 4+rlogis(mysampsize)
Z17 <- rgamma(mysampsize,1.5)
Z18 <- rf(mysampsize,20,10)
Z19 <- 2 + 3*runif(mysampsize)
Z20 <- rnorm(mysampsize,2,1) + rnorm(mysampsize,3,2)
```

We ask readers that if you use this dataset, you cite this chapter.

REFERENCES

Anderson, E. T., & Simester, D. (2011). A step-by-step guide to smart business experiments. *Harvard Business Review,* March, 98–105

Burke, J. F., Sussman, J. B., Kent, D. M., & Hayward, R. A. (2015). *Three simple rules to ensure reasonably credible subgroup analyses.* doi:10.1136/bmj.h5651

Fayers, P. M., & King, M. T. (2009). How to guarantee finding a statistically significant difference: The use and abuse of subgroup analyses. *Quality of Life Research, 18*(5), 527–530. doi:10.1007/s11136-009-9473-3

Mitsnefes, M. M., Khoury, P. R., & Devarajan, P. (2008). Beware of subgroup analysis. *Pediatric Nephrology, 23*(7), 1191–1192. doi:10.1007/s00467-008-0791-4

Naggara, O., Raymond, J., Guilbert, F., & Altman, D. G. (2011). The problem of subgroup analyses: An example from a trial on ruptured intracranial aneurysms. *American Journal of Neuroradiology, 32*(4), 633–636. doi:10.3174/ajnr.a2442

Oxman, A. D., & Guyatt, G. H. (1992). A consumer's guide to subgroup analyses. *Annals of Internal Medicine, 116*(1), 78–84. doi:10.7326/0003-4819-116-1-78

Peto, R. (1990). Misleading subgroup analyses in GISSI. *The American Journal of Cardiology, 66*(7), 771. doi:10.1016/0002-9149(90)91149-z

Peto, R. (2005). Similarities and differences between adjuvant hormonal therapy in breast and prostate cancer. *Prostate Cancer Update, 4*(1), 9–11.

Rothwell, P. M. (2005). Subgroup analysis in randomised controlled trials: Importance, indications, and interpretation. *The Lancet, 365*(9454), 176–186. doi:10.1016/s0140-6736(05)17709-5

Sun, X., Briel, M., Busse, J. W., You, J., Akl, E., Mejza, F., . . . Guyatt, G. (2012). Credibility of claims of subgroup effects in randomised controlled trials: Systematic review. *The Spine Journal, 12*(7), 635. doi:10.1016/j.spinee.2012.07.029

Varadhan, R, & Seeger, J. D. (2013). Estimation and reporting of heterogeneity of treatment effects. In P. Velentgas, N. A. Dreyer, & P. Nourjah (Eds.), *Developing a protocol for observational comparative effectiveness research: A user's guide* (pp. 35–44). Washington, DC: Agency for Healthcare Research and Quality.

CHAPTER 7

BUSINESS INTELLIGENCE CHALLENGES FOR SMALL AND MEDIUM-SIZED BUSINESS

Leveraging Existing Resources

Nick Perrino, Gregory Smith, David Hyland, and Mark Frolick
Xavier University

ABSTRACT

Small and medium businesses (SMEs) face many unique challenges with business intelligence (BI) initiatives when compared to larger firms. Unfortunately for SMEs, the largest barrier to entry is often the lack of financial resources. However with proper planning and support, an SME can have fruitful BI initiative implementations. To aid in this discovery, this article introduces a five-step, success driven plan for SMEs to approach BI without the need for the investment of resources enjoyed by large enterprises. By simply identifying problems correctly, discovering what data a company is capturing and mining, choosing key performance indicators (KPIs), and training employees to implement the program, any company can have successful BI initiatives, including SMEs.

Contemporary Perspectives on Data Mining, Volume 3, pages 93–102

Small businesses play a substantial role in the American economic system. According to the U.S. Small Business Administration (SBA), small businesses account for 54% of all sales in the United States and 55% of jobs in the U.S. economy. According to the SBA, there are approximately 28 million small businesses currently operating in the United States (Baer, Ariyachandra, & Frolick, 2013) with one small business existing for every 11 people. In order for these small businesses to be successful, it is important that they leverage the data that is produced in the course of business activity.

WHAT IS BUSINESS INTELLIGENCE?

Survival in the modern age of business has shifted from experiential reasoning to empirical analysis of situations. In the past, business leaders looked to experience when dealing with unknown situations. Fortunately, technology has seen a great leap forward over the last three decades, including the advent of modern *business intelligence* (BI). BI is an umbrella term that encompasses a wealth of information systems used to collect, manage, and "analyze complex information about an organization and its competitors for use in business planning and decision making" (Frolick & von Oven, 2005). For many years, large businesses have been implementing BI programs. As a result, business intelligence is becoming ubiquitous in large corporations, favoring those with large budgets and the capability to access and pay skilled workforces. BI as a market has substantially grown thanks to the general acceptance by most major multinational corporations. An analysis of the BI industry by Louis Columbus for *Forbes* magazine showed strong rapid growth and acceptance over the past two decades. The *Forbes* study found that "89% of business leaders believe Big Data will revolutionize business operations in the same way the Internet did" (Columbus, 2015). In addition, businesses that sell data analytic tools continue to see massive growth. Wikibon's projections for the Big Data market show that the industry will grow from $7.6 billion to over $84 billion by 2026. The problem, however, is that some of the most popular BI tools are incredibly expensive to purchase and maintain (Columbus, 2015). This leaves smaller companies at a competitive disadvantage since they do not have large IT budgets to pay for expensive tools and workers.

WHY DO SMALL BUSINESSES STRUGGLE WITH BI?

Success in BI is often difficult for small businesses. The struggles emanate from two areas. First, small businesses generally have a limited number of employees and need to prioritize primary business functions, which make it difficult to focus on business intelligence. This does not allow for full participation in the idea of using technology and data to leverage insights and make decisions (Edala, 2012). These businesses fail to either fully benefit from the BI systems purchased or refuse to invest their resources in the systems because the risk is too high. A recent survey found that obtaining clearer insights with the organization remains a significant challenge for small companies and these companies will therefore be less likely to use or plan to use analytics/mining solutions (Baer et al., 2013).

The second BI struggle comes from businesses buying into the appeal of services that guarantee managers the opportunity to access a wealth of data and information that can aid in several sectors of their existing businesses. These companies can often falter in their BI initiatives, as they are paralyzed by the influx of information and shortage of skilled workers and employees who can truly manipulate data to draw value-added insights and conclusions (Bison Analytics, 2016). This creates a need for an effective plan for small businesses to embrace business intelligence.

FIVE STEPS TO EFFECTIVELY IMPLEMENT A BI STRATEGY IN A SMALL BUSINESS

If the goal for any small business is to effectively take advantage of BI tools, then it must approach the realm of BI in a realistic manner. Necessary to this are five key steps that small businesses must follow when beginning a BI initiative. These steps can be found in Figure 7.1. The first and most important step in beginning a BI initiative is to identify a problem or area of need. Second, it is beneficial to identify any current BI tools that may already exist within the company. This may mean identifying sources of data or functions within programs already owned. The third step is to identify key performance indicators (KPIs), which give insights into the areas of need based on data available. KPIs are quantifiable measures of a company's performance in specific areas of the business (Investopedia, n.d.). Fourth, if the KPIs or information needed for solving a specific problem cannot be handled through existing technology, the company must look externally for tools and services that can aid in achieving a specific goal. The fifth and final step for small business to initiate BI is to implement these BI systems in problem-solving situations. In conjunction with this final step resides one of the most important parts of implementing BI tools: employee buy-in. Employees at all levels of the firm must be on board with the BI project. This is essential to the overall accuracy and success of implementing a BI system.

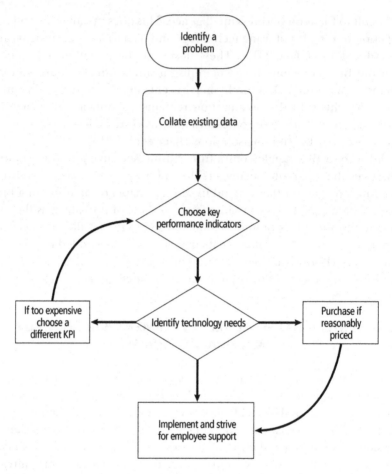

Figure 7.1 Five steps for business intelligence implementation for small and medium enterprises.

Step 1: Identify the Problem

Problem identification requires two realizations. First, business intelligence tools, as an asset, are problem specific. Christopher Null points out that companies should simply identify a singular problem and explore related data for insights (Null, 2013). Companies must also ensure that BI tools are not being purchased blindly, but rather purchased to serve specific needs within the organization. A blind leap into BI systems may create waste by purchasing tools that may never be used. In addition, companies that isolate singular problems can effectively target those areas with a limited number of specific tools and systems. Not only will this reduce waste, but it will give employees an opportunity to utilize these programs more efficiently since they can focus on one or two applications directly related to a specific problem.

Reinvesting limited resources back into small businesses means that each penny spent for BI services or tools must be aimed toward something that adds value. Identifying a problem or area of need first will ensure resources are efficiently allocated, and that the BI system will be used in a manner that promotes the overall success of the business. The value of the BI system, in its inherent ability, is to aid the user with a specific goal. Belicove emphasizes the need for a company to begin with one specific problem or goal in mind as an important starting point for gathering data within a company. It is hard to know what data is or is not relevant without having these specific goals in mind. By identifying a specific goal or problem, the company can begin to research what data is needed for analysis in solving the identified problem (Belicove, 2013).

Step 2: Use What You Have

Once the problem has been determined, a company must identify and leverage existing data and tools. In an attempt to limit a company's initial investment and avoid the "all-in pitfall" in a BI system, it is important to recognize that most companies, even SMEs, have a great deal of existing data. Identifying key sources of data within the company and then matching it with relevant problems and goals is a great way to leverage existing data that was previously thought to be complicated or unimportant.

Skiles states that the first step to leveraging existing data is to gather information from multiple internal sources and begin to understand what data is available for analysis (Skiles, 2014). An important point to consider is that one must be fully confident in the data that has been collected. It is widely known that for any data analysis to occur, data sources need to be refined and reviewed to ensure that the information is true before moving forward (Belicove, 2013).

Building on this, it is essential that a trusted data source be the foundation for data governance. Data governance can be defined as "the policies, rules, standards, definitions, stewardship, and enforcement required to ensure that an organization and its processes and infra-structures best support the effective use of high-quality data in achieving corporate goals and objectives" (Page, 2011).

Data governance is essential for success and must be strictly followed at all levels of an organization. Page states that "data governance is about making sure everyone working with business intelligence is empowered, capable, and enthused to do their jobs and contribute to your enterprise's success"

(Page, 2011, p. 24). Small businesses must recognize that data governance policies should be rooted from the bottom up, where business intelligence users operate on the ground (bottom) level and work to identify where data governance policies are needed (Page, 2011, p. 21). That way SMEs may allocate limited resources to data governance only where necessary.

Step 3: Identify Key Performance Indicators (KPIs)

Once decision makers have a grasp on what data is available through existing channels, it is important to decide which key performance indicators (KPIs) should be reported and tracked. KPIs are important success measures as they are based on the organization's individual strategy and plan for success. Once a company decides what the overall goals are, and establishes the methods by which they will go about achieving those goals, then appropriate KPIs can be chosen (Worth, 2016). KPIs serve as an important snapshot of the progress being made by different sectors within the organization. When using KPIs, great care should be given to "monitor change as close to real time as possible and hold people accountable for improvements" (Worth, 2016).

While there are many KPIs that can be monitored, business leaders should focus on those KPIs that are easily calculated based on data attained simply from existing resources. Building on this, SAP identifies several key KPIs that small businesses should focus on. They serve as good examples of indicators that do not rely on an overbearing amount of data and can serve as vital performance measures for decision makers. The first is the *cash flow forecast* (Equation 7.1).

$$\text{Cash Flow Forecast} = \text{Total Cash in Bank} + \text{Projected Cash In} - \text{Projected Cash Out}^1 \qquad (7.1)$$

The cash flow forecast allows business leaders to identify potential shortages in cash. This is even more critical for small businesses, which have limited income channels. More importantly, this information can easily be found through historical sales records based on time of year and liquid asset reports from a company's accounting department (Concur Team, 2014)

Another measure is *gross profit margin* (Equation 7.2) as a percentage of sales.

$$\text{Gross Profit Margin} = (\text{Revenue} - \text{Cost of Goods Sold})/\text{Revenue} \qquad (7.2)$$

This KPI only requires users to know the selling price and cost of goods that are sold, as well as total sales. This allows them to identify the margins between what they are selling goods for versus what price goods are being purchased at. This KPI, although simple in its calculation, gives small business leaders the power to leverage their understanding of their company's performance when negotiating the price of goods being purchased from suppliers.

Step 4: Need It, Get It

If the KPIs that align most with the goals of the business require data and/or tools not currently available from existing sources, then the firm must look externally for help. Completing the first three steps prior to shopping for external BI software will allow a company to focus only on those programs that serve a specific need. This allows companies to focus on limited resources and avoid the risk of over buying.

Step 5: Implementation and Employee Buy-In

Once a small business has decided on a problem to investigate, mined for existing data, picked KPIs, and found any added outside resources, it can then move onto the implementation stage. Successful implementation relies on two important parts. The first part is employee training and familiarization with the importance of the BI initiative. Second comes the ability to observe the BI program along with its successes and shortcomings while operating the program. An open line of communication from all parties will allow for corrections and adjustments to be made when needed to promote the overall success of the BI program.

Employee buy-in is important for all realms of business, but is quintessential for business intelligence. Employees at the ground level of any business are going to engage with customers and ultimately be responsible for proper customer interaction and appropriate data collection. Ensuring that employees are able to use the BI tools, understand the importance of data accuracy, and the impact of the KPIs created will allow the BI initiative to move forward smoothly. A recent study on BI found that an "awareness of the significance of the new Information System in assisting employees in their daily tasks would make them more receptive toward Information System innovation capability" (Ainin, Salleh, Bahri, & Faziharudean, 2015). The authors of this study concluded that employees who lack the necessary training on a specific BI initiative may also lack the necessary confidence to participate as fully engaged members of the program. These employees ultimately create a gap between the decision maker, the BI program, and the end customer. With this comes an obvious loss in customer value from the failure of the program to operate as it was designed (Ainin, et al., 2015). Therefore, it is logical to conclude that employee buy-in and proper training on how they can effectively execute their necessary duties should be considered a top priority during this phase.

Once implemented, BI program leaders should be receptive to feedback and reviews of the program from all three of the major parties—employee, decision maker, and customer—as they look to understand how successful the program is in problem solving or generating necessary insights into a specific area of the business. This idea of user feedback was detailed in a study done involving the implementation of BI tools in any organization; it found feedback allowed decision makers to identify the source of a problem and possibly fix or adapt it even more to the business (Kirby & Robinson, 2009). The BI team within any company should focus on the small scale initiative it started with and then adapt to meet new and larger challenges. By expanding slowly, a team can avoid the all-in pitfall by only adding tools as needed and not wasting time on events that are not a priority to the business and its overall BI strategy.

CONCLUSION

A recent article estimates that nearly 90% of all data currently saved in databases and being analyzed had been created in the last two years (Belicove, 2013). Companies can no longer ignore the fact that data and BI initiatives are drivers in decision making for modern businesses no matter the size of a company. However, small businesses need to approach business intelligence implementation with caution.

The two major pitfalls, the all-in and no-BI strategies, have proven unsuccessful in promoting BI success for small businesses. The world is increasingly becoming technologically driven. Small businesses must participate in BI initiatives to put themselves in a position to be successful like larger corporations. Companies must identify specific instances where BI tools can be used to gain leverage, and identify what data and tools they have and need. This data can then be used to produce measures of relevant statistical information that business leaders can use to make valuable insights. Once selected, an implementation strategy that focuses on employee empowerment, training, and feedback will allow even the smallest businesses to leverage data and information, which may have previously gone unused.

NOTE

1. The actual cash flow calculation in practice might involve many sources of projected cash inflows and many sources of cash outflows. Cash flow forecast-

ing and monitoring is particularly important for small businesses as many find that as they grow they are profitable but due to reinvest in the business and working capital they are not having the cash to stay solvent. Note that the measures used here are very basic to illustrate things that are important for all businesses. More advanced KPIs could be used based on the specific business.

REFERENCES

Ainin, S., Salleh, N. A., Bahri, S., & Faziharudean, T. M. (2015). Organization's performance, customer value and the functional capabilities of information systems. *Information Systems Management, 32*(1), 2–14. doi:10.1080/10580530.2015.983012

Baer, M., Ariyachandra, T., & Frolick, M. (2013, November). Initiating and implementing data mining practices within a small to medium-sized business organization. *Journal of Economics, Business and Management,* 334–338. doi:10.7763/joebm.2013.v1.72

Belicove, M. E. (2013, May). Discovering the buried treasure. *Entrepreneur, 41*(5), 1–40.

Bison Analytics. (2016). *The biggest issue in implementing BI for small business.* Retrieved August 5, 2016, from https://bisonanalytics.com/blog/biggest-issue-implementing-business-intelligence-for-small-business/?nabe=4853591734484992:1

Columbus, L. (2015, May 25). *Roundup of analytics, big data & business intelligence forecasts and market estimates.* Retrieved July 10, 2016, from http://www.forbes.com/sites/louiscolumbus/2015/05/25/roundup-of-analytics-big-data-business-intelligence-forecasts-and-market-estimates-2015/#40b4157d4869

Concur Team. (2014, November 13). *Monitor these 5 KPIs to keep your small business in the black.* Retrieved June 21, 2016, from https://www.concur.com/newsroom/article/5-essential-small-business-kpis-to-monitor_13nov2014_sb

Edala, S. (2012, December 28). *Big data analytics: Not just for big business anymore* (E. Savitz, Ed.). Retrieved August 5, 2016, from http://www.forbes.com/sites/ciocentral/2012/12/28/big-data-analytics-not-just-for-big-business-anymore/#1521797cd3ae

Frolick, M. N., & von Oven, M. (2006). Taking the repetition out of research and development: The BI collaboration approach. *Business Intelligence Journal, 11*(3), 21.

Investopedia. (n.d.). *Key performance indicators: KPI.* (2015). Retrieved June 21, 2016, from http://www.investopedia.com/terms/k/kpi.asp

Kirby, S., & Robertson, B. (2009, January). Start small and build toward business intelligence. *Healthcare Financial Management, 1*(96), 103.

Null, C. (2013, August 27). *How small businesses can mine big data.* Retrieved August 5, 2016, from http://www.pcworld.com/article/2047486/how-small-businesses-can-mine-big-data.html

Page, J. (2011). How to launch a data governance initiative. *Business Intelligence Journal, 16*(2), 17–25.

Skiles, D. (2014, February 24). *Even small firms can use big data.* Retrieved July 21, 2016, from http://www.thinkadvisor.com/2014/02/24/even-small-firms-can -use-big-data

Worth, J. (2016, May 5). *The best way to track your company's performance.* Retrieved July 21, 2016, from https://www.entrepreneur.com/article/273484

SECTION III

TOPICS IN DATA MINING

CHAPTER 8

DATA MINING TECHNIQUES APPLIED TO OUTCOME ANALYSIS AND VALIDATION FOR THE FUTURES DRUG AND ALCOHOL REHABILITATION CENTER

Virginia Miori and Catherine Cardamone
Saint Joseph's University

ABSTRACT

Alcohol and substance abuse rehabilitation centers must face the challenge of validating outcomes to meet the burden of evidence for insurance companies. In particular, treatment success rates have a direct impact on a patient's ability to receive insurance coverage for treatment programs. In this chapter we specifically examine Futures of Palm Beach, a rehabilitation center. Data collected include admissions, satisfaction surveys, postdischarge surveys, medical histories, and demographics. Data mining and statistical techniques including clustering, partitioning, ANOVA (analysis of variance), stepwise re-

Contemporary Perspectives on Data Mining, Volume 3, pages 105–133
Copyright © 2018 by Information Age Publishing

gression, and stepwise logistic regression are applied to the data to determine statistically significant drivers of treatment success.

According to the CDC (2016), the crude death rate (Figure 8.1) due to substance and alcohol abuse has increased from 13.8 deaths per 100,000 population in 1999, to 25.2 deaths per 100,000 population in 2014. This increase of over 82% highlights the importance of care and treatment for addicted individuals. In the face of this devastating statistic, the Futures of Palm Beach rehabilitation center is one of many centers striving to provide effective treatment for the diseases of alcoholism and addiction.

Ultimately, the success that Futures experiences will be based on their ability to not only treat addiction, but to also demonstrate successful outcomes. Futures has collected data from multiple sources to develop an understanding of its client base, the needs of its clients, and the critical success factors in treatment supporting analysis of outcomes.

The first client touchpoint is a phone call or a web inquiry with a responding phone call. Admitted clients receive treatment and may elect to leave before treatment completion. Upon discharge, clients are given recommendations for moving forward. A change in geography and living situation may be suggested, and all clients are encouraged to remain in outpatient care, attend meetings, and stay in contact with the alumni organization.

During the first call, the nature of the addiction is recorded and a short medical history is taken. Once a client is admitted into the facility, further demographic and medical information is collected in the electronic medical records.

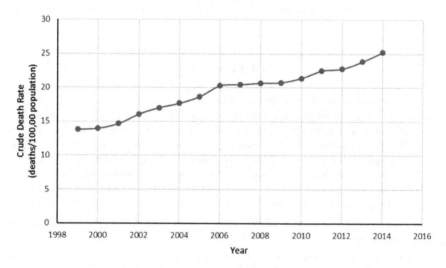

Figure 8.1 CDC reported deaths due to substance and alcohol abuse.

Insurance approval is provided at multiple points throughout client treatment. Each progressive phase of treatment requires approval. These approvals typically support 5 to 10 days of treatment, necessitating multiple approvals through every client treatment program. Insurance collections and cash collections are accumulated over the course of the client's residence and for up to six months after their discharge. Should insurance be declined for any phase of treatment, clients are retained until treatment completion (a commitment made at their admission). The only possible exception exists when an insurance carrier is particularly aggressive and forces a client to be transferred to an alternate facility. Clients with these carriers would be informed at the outset of this possibility. Note that clients may also choose to pay for treatment out of their own pockets.

The primary therapeutic methodology used at Futures is dialectic behavior therapy (DBT). This therapy is effective in treating a dual diagnosis of mental health disorders and substance abuse disorders. This therapy addresses the core emotional level and the practical level (coping skills). DBT is combined with individual therapy, as emotional regulation program, family program, wellness program, meal planning and support, relapse prevention, and life satisfaction programs (Futures, 2016).

Upon discharge from the facility, each client is asked to complete a satisfaction survey. After discharge, data on substance use and life experiences are collected at specified intervals (7 days, 30 days, 60 days, 120 days, etc.) In addition to data collection at Futures, death rate data are collected from the Centers for Disease Control.

LITERATURE SURVEY

Limited statistically significant research on outcomes in substance and alcohol abuse has been completed. Original studies are completed and ultimately combined with other studies and then examined. This literature review examines these studies along with articles quantifying the pervasiveness of addiction and approaches to limited relapses.

Substance and alcohol abuse have become rampant in American society. Though not all cases of abuse result in addiction or abusive use of substances, one-third of people between the ages of 18 and 25 have admitted to binge drinking, while one-fifth have admitted to using illicit drugs (SAHMSA, 2014). The demand for rehabilitation centers has increased accordingly. The primary challenge facing these centers is that of verifying outcomes. One result of this increase will be the reliance on clinical outcomes for behavioral health income (Bithoney, 2016). Better results at lower costs will then be rewarded.

The number of facilities treating alcohol and substance abuse doubled between 1980 and 1994 (Heinrich & Fornier, 2004). Private, for-profit facilities are also on the rise. The chance of relapse is influenced by age, previous treatment, and length of time in treatment, though additional treatment time has a negative impact on employment prospects. A series of factors relating to relapse after treatment are associated with managed care, parent organizations, and a perceived loss of autonomy (Ghose, 2008). JCAHO (Joint Commission on the Accreditation of Healthcare Organizations) accredited facilities are found to reduce the risk of relapse.

Immediate insurance verification has been instituted for Florida drug and alcohol rehabilitation centers, along with a formula to customize treatments ensuring success rates at twice the national average (PRWeb, 2016). Private insurance is found to limit follow-up services, increasing the chance of relapse (Ali & Mutter, 2016). Long-term outcomes in methadone maintenance programs have suffered from nonresponse bias and self-reporting bias, limiting the use of the results (Bovass & Cacciola, 2003).

Studies have examined characteristics of substance abusers. Gender differences have been explored extensively (Yih-Ing, Yu-Chuang, Teruya, & Anglin, 2004) and though consistent conclusions of differences between treatment outcomes have not been established, men and women do have different recovery experiences. Women begin using later in life and are prone to use cocaine and crack. Men begin earlier and tend toward alcohol and heroin.

The differences between ethnicity and race have been examined through clinical trials (Milligan, Nich, & Carroll, 2004). The method of administration differs by races along with some drugs of choice. African Americans have a lower probability of remaining in treatment when compared to Caucasians. Study results have concluded that limited differences exist between races, and the overall goal should be to increase retention rates in rehabilitation facilities. Attitudes toward race within rehabilitation centers were found to be biased in a manner consistent with ethnic stereotypes (Nielson, Bonn, & Wilson, 2010).

The communication approach to health care was adapted for use in rehabilitation centers and outcomes (Jesus & Silva, 2016). Using the four rehab communication elements is a superior choice. These include building a supportive relationship, effective information exchange, goal setting, and fostering a positive attitude. This approach can be adapted to different patients with different characteristics. Focus on the treatment process and communication was argued as being preferable to examination of outcomes (Simpson, 2004), with more focus placed on how treatment works and how it can be improved.

Prize-based contingency management was found to be effective in avoiding relapse in an examination of 18 studies (Benishek et al., 2014). Results were not statistically significant, and relapses did, however, occur after treatment ended. Enhanced incentives were examined in a study of 21 dually diagnosed veterans (current psychiatric and substance/alcohol dependence) and yielded promising results (Drebing et al., 2005). The enhanced incentive group was able to meet its goals more rapidly leading to a faster job search and decreased chance of relapse.

DATA PREPARATION

Data Collection

Preadmissions contact records are stored within the customer relationship management (CRM) system (Salesforce). Data collection reflects clients admitted beginning February 2014 through May 2016. Once clients are admitted, this system holds general medical history responses, demographic and address information, and insurance information. Salesforce provides direct extract capabilities allowing this data to be exported to Microsoft Excel.

In-patient data were collected from the electronic medical records (EMR) system (KIPU), including additional demographic information, diagnosis codes, and phases of treatment from February 2014 to May 2016. Though KIPU is meant to maintain an export to Microsoft Excel, it was not functional; therefore, data collection required page-by-page copy and paste of the report pages processed into a document.

The satisfaction survey in use by Futures was redesigned at the start of data collection for this paper. The survey was provided to each client (on paper) upon their discharge. Data from this survey was collected by the clinical staff from January 2016 to May 2016 at the Futures rehabilitation facility and stored in a Microsoft Excel file. This Excel file was augmented with limited demographic data as well as responses to all survey questions. The survey had 23 varying Likert scale questions, 1 binary response question, and 5 open response questions. The responses to the five open questions were stored in their own data file in preparation for text mining.

The post discharge survey was conducted at 7 days, 30 days, 60 days, 90 days, 6 months, 12 months, and 18 months after discharge. Data was collected from February 2014 to May 2016. Surveys of this nature are prone to induce shame in respondents, therefore contact was made by phone with a softened approach to each question. These surveys were conducted by trained Futures rehabilitation alumni to further increase frequency of responses and the likelihood of accurate responses. The postdischarge survey focused on use of substances, required medical attention, and family and living conditions. The survey contained 14 binary response questions, and 5 scaled questions. As part of this paper, the survey was redesigned to collect more comprehensive responses. The redesign included 10 scaled questions, 9 binary questions and 5 free response questions.

The Centers for Disease Control and Prevention (CDC, 2016) data were collected in order to examine Futures's data in the context of national data on alcohol and substance abuse.

Data Cleaning

Before aggregating data into a single file for analysis, extensive cleaning was required. Though the systems used to collect data were standardized systems, data entry conventions had not been institutionalized, nor had they been built into the software interfaces. The data issues fell into four distinct categories: incorrect data, inaccurate data, missing data, and poorly formatted data.

Incorrect data refers to data that was accumulated but verifiably incorrect. It may not be the result of intentional false reporting by potential clients, faulty recollections from potential clients under the influence, or even poor cellphone connections. Unlike other health care settings, initial client contact with alcohol and substance abuse rehabilitation centers do not carry the incentive for complete honesty. Inaccurate data, however was the result of typographical errors and inconsistencies in data input. These errors included mistyping the zip code, not knowing or selecting the wrong state abbreviation, entering a state name rather than a state abbreviation, and lack of consistency with middle names and name suffixes (i.e., Jr. versus Jr) among many other typos.

Missing data have multiple possible causes. In the case of data input from calls to admissions counselors, potential clients may be unwilling to provide all the information requested. Admissions counselors may not understand all of the responses provided by a caller under the influence. Rather than inputing potentially incorrect information, they leave the field blank. Once individuals are clients of the facility, a lack of uniformity in fields entered into the EMR is documented. Finally, not all clients respond to surveys, resulting in missing survey data.

The final culprit in the creation of a significant data cleaning need is poorly (inconsistently) formatted data. Open response fields for drug of choice (primary, secondary, and tertiary) and for diagnosis codes are processed differently by different parties entering the data. Some may use a space as a delimiter between discrete pieces of information, while others use commas. Diagnosis codes are not consistently applied and may be omitted, leaving only the verbal description of the diagnosis.

Extensive data cleaning was performed to rectify all errors that could be verified as incorrect. This cleaning was performed manually, aided by functions within Microsoft Excel and relational matching in Microsoft Access.

Data Aggregation

Data from the multiple sources were aggregated into two distinct analysis files. The first of these files included a single record for each client's stay at the Futures rehabilitation center. The second file included multiple records for each client stay at Futures, reflecting responses from the same client, from after the associated stay to the postdischarge survey. It is not uncommon for a client to relapse and return to the center. These stays were treated separately.

DATA ANALYSIS

Data analysis was performed using Microsoft Excel, Tableau, SAS JMP and Stata software. Each tool provided unique capabilities that enhanced the analysis. The goals of the analysis were (a) to understand the client population and the factors that led to successful completion of a rehabilitation program; (b) understand the effectiveness of aspects of facility and treatment based on client survey responses; and (c) to understand the factors that led to clients' ability to remain sober after their departure from the center.

Completion of a rehabilitation program is not merely determined by the number of days spent at a rehabilitation facility. Each client undergoes a tailored program to meet his or her needs and it is approved in stages by the insurance company. The ideal case is that discharge from the center will occur at completion of treatment. Discharge may also be administrative, medical administrative, against medical advice, and other. The frequency of each type of discharge is presented in Figure 8.2.

Over 69% of clients are discharged at completion of treatment; 20.5% of clients depart against medical advice; and almost 8% are administratively discharged. The mean of days in treatment is 24.5 days with a standard deviation of 10.15 days; 68% of clients stayed between 25 and 35 days. The median length of stay was 29 days; 20% of clients leave before 15 days of treatment. Figure 8.3 shows the days in treatment for the three primary discharge types by gender. Figure 8.4 shows average days in treatment by (three primary) discharge types by age group. Figure 8.5 provides days in treatment by primary drug of choice. Finally, Table 8.1a and 8.1b includes percent of discharge type for each opportunity owner. (Names have been replaced with generic indicators.) Table 8.1a accumulates discharge type percentages across opportunity owner (column based); Table 8.1b accumulates discharge type percentages by opportunity owner (row based).

Table 8.2a provides a summary of significant demographic variable single factor ANOVA results with days in treatment as a response variable. Table 8.2b provides a summary of significant satisfaction survey response

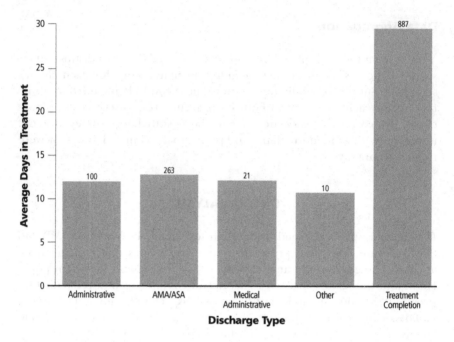

Figure 8.2 Futures discharge type.

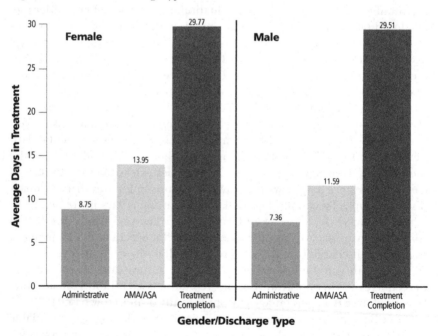

Figure 8.3 Average days in treatment by gender and discharge type.

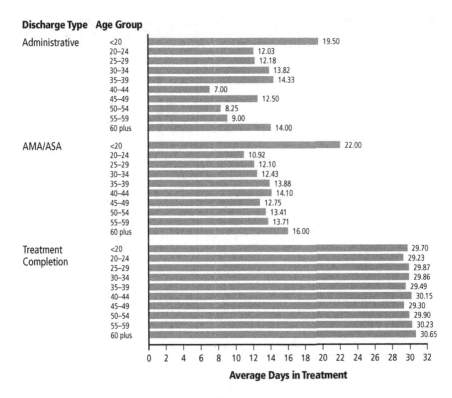

Figure 8.4 Days in treatment by age group and discharge type.

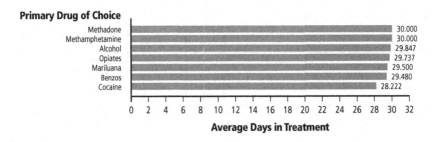

Figure 8.5 Days in treatment by primary drug of choice.

single factor ANOVA results. Basic demographic information provided few significant or meaningful findings. The satisfaction survey did however yield more significant and actionable results. The satisfaction Likert scale had six possible responses ranging from very dissatisfied to very satisfied. All ANOVA results are available upon request from the authors.

TABLE 8.1a	Discharge Type Percentages Across Opportunity Owner				
	Discharge Type				
Opportunity Owner: Full Name	Administrative	AMA/ASA	Medical Administrative	Other	Treatment Completion
Owner 1	2.00%	3.80%	4.76%		6.20%
Owner 2					0.34%
Owner 3	2.00%	2.28%		10.00%	2.25%
Owner 4	7.00%	10.27%	4.76%	10.00%	7.22%
Owner 5	2.00%	3.42%		10.00%	2.82%
Owner 6	9.00%	6.46%	9.52%		6.43%
Owner 7		0.38%			0.23%
Owner 8	6.00%	4.94%	14.29%	10.00%	6.54%
Owner 9	17.00%	14.07%	4.76%	20.00%	14.09%
Owner 10	11.00%	7.22%	19.05%	10.00%	11.05%
Owner 11					0.11%
Owner 12	6.00%	8.37%	4.76%		7.33%
Owner 13	10.00%	9.89%	4.76%		7.10%
Owner 14	5.00%	6.08%			5.41%
Owner 15	1.00%	0.38%	4.76%		1.24%
Owner 16	1.00%	6.46%			4.06%
Owner 17	4.00%	1.90%	4.76%		2.14%
Owner 18	2.00%	1.14%			1.69%
Owner 19		0.38%	9.52%		0.23%
Owner 20	3.00%	6.08%	9.52%	10.00%	4.74%
Owner 21	2.00%	1.14%		10.00%	2.48%
Owner 22	10.00%	5.32%	4.76%	10.00%	6.31%
Total	100.00%	100.00%	100.00%	100.00%	100.00%

Hierarchical clustering and K Means clustering on the independent variables—days in treatment, age, cash collections, and insurance collections—were set to produce five clusters (Figures 8.6 and 8.7). In the case of K Means, a single outlier became its own cluster. Of the four remaining clusters, one held client with stays averaging just over 8 days. Three clusters were comprised of clients who all stayed for 28 to 29 days, but were distinguished by their age, cash collections, and insurance collections. Figure 8.6

TABLE 8.1b	Discharge Type Percentages for Each Opportunity Owner					
	Discharge Type					
Opportunity Owner: Full Name	Administrative	AMA/ASA	Medical Administrative	Other	Treatment Completion	Total
Owner 1	2.94%	14.71%	1.47		80.88%	100.00%
Owner 2					100.00%	100.00%
Owner 3	6.90%	20.69%		3.45%	68.97%	100.00%
Owner 4	7.00%	27.00%	1.00%	1.00%	64.00%	100.00%
Owner 5	5.41%	24.32%		2.70%	67.57%	100.00%
Owner 6	10.59%	20.00%	2.35%		67.06%	100.00%
Owner 7		33.33%			66.67%	100.00%
Owner 8	7.41%	16.05%	3.70%	1.23%	71.60%	100.00%
Owner 9	9.34%	20.33%	0.55%	1.10%	68.68%	100.00%
Owner 10	8.27%	14.29%	3.01%	0.75%	73.68%	100.00%
Owner 11					100.00%	100.00%
Owner 12	6.38%	23.40%	1.06%		69.15%	100.00%
Owner 13	10.00%	26.00%	1.00%		63.00%	100.00%
Owner 14	7.25%	23.19%			69.57%	100.00%
Owner 15	7.14%	7.14%	7.14%		78.57%	100.00%
Owner 16	1.85%	31.48%			66.67%	100.00%
Owner 17	13.79%	17.24%	3.45%		65.52%	100.00%
Owner 18	10.00%	15.00%			75.00%	100.00%
Owner 19		20.00%	40.00%		40.00%	100.00%
Owner 20	4.69%	25.00%	3.13%	1.56%	65.63%	100.00%
Owner 21	7.14%	10.71%		3.57%	78.57%	100.00%
Owner 22	12.20%	17.07%	1.22%	1.22%	68.29%	100.00%
Total	7.81%	20.53%	1.64%	0.78%	69.24%	100.00%

shows that a total of 890 clients fell into these three clusters: 318 clients, with an average age of 51.00 years, relied heavily (93.9%) on insurance collections; 145 clients, with an average age of 42.77 years, had minimal reliance (4.7%) on insurance collections, paying the significant majority of their treatment out of their own pockets. The final cluster of 427 clients had an average age of 26.77 years and again relied heavily on insurance collections (94.5%) to cover the cost of treatment.

TABLE 8.2a Significant Factor Differences for Days in Treatment			
Factor	Significant Pairs	Difference (days)	p-vaule
Age group	40–49 versus 25–29	4.75	0.0074
	55–59 versus 25–29	4.49	0.0243
Gender	Males versus Females	−1.97	0.0017
Marital status	Divorced versus Single	3.54	0.0223
Discharge type	Treatment Completion versus Administrative	17.74	<0.0001
	Treatment Completion versus Medical Administrative	17.61	<0.0001
	Treatment Completion versus AMA/ASA	16.92	<0.0001
Primary drug of choice	Alcohol versus Opiates	3.53	0.0057

The results of the hierarchical clustering (Figures 8.8 and 8.9) again

TABLE 8.2b Significant Satisfaction Survey Factors for Days in Treatment			
Factor	Significant Pairs	Difference (days)	p-vaule
Experience with medical staff (first 48 hours)	Mod D versus Very D	7.00	0.0038
	Mod D versus Slight S	6.67	0.0005
	Mod D versus Mod S	6.52	0.0003
	Mod D versus Ext S	6.32	0.0003
Experience with medical administration	Mod D versus Very D	3.89	0.0101
	Mod D versus Slight S	3.33	0.0268
	Mod D versus Ext S	3.12	0.0194
Satisfaction with setting treatment goals	Slight L versus Slight H	7.25	<0.0001
	Slight L versus Mod H	6.89	<0.0001
	Slight L versus Very H	6.85	<0.0001
Treatment by admissions staff	Slight D versus Slight S	15.83	<0.0001
	Slight D versus Very D	15.00	<0.0001
	Slight D versus Mod S	14.38	<0.0001
	Slight D versus Ext S	14.22	<0.0001
	Ext S versus Slight S	1.61	0.0394
Treatment by RA staff	Mod D versus Very D	4.60	0.0015
	Slight S versus Very D	3.22	0.0147
	Ext S versus Very D	2.94	0.0158
	Mod S versus Very D	2.83	0.0268

⊿ ⬇ **K Means NCluster=5**

Columns Scaled Individually

⊿ **Cluster Summary**

Cluster	Count	Step	Criterion
1	249	20	0
2	318		
3	145		
4	427		
5	1		

⊿ **Cluster Means**

Cluster	Days in Treatment	Age	Cash Collections	Insurance Collections
1	8.13253012	32.6827309	1811.39863	5510.30116
2	28.9968553	50.9654088	1668.61909	25467.9565
3	28.2413793	42.7724138	27569.8879	1364.32717
4	28.8969555	26.7728337	1404.86375	24263.9522
5	81	38	34151	16325

Figure 8.6   K Means Cluster summary.

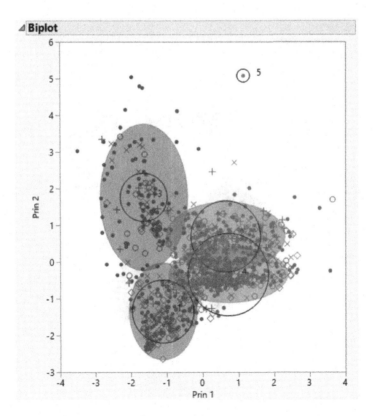

Figure 8.7   K Means Cluster biplot.

produced one cluster with just over 8 days average spent in treatment. The remaining clusters highlighted two groups with very high total collections and very low total collections. Both groups remained in care for the entire program (27.7 days and 30.3 days) with total collections of $15,755 and $49,605 compared to an overall average of $22,508. The final two groups reflected clients with very high or very low insurance collections (93.4% and 3.4%).

⊿ Cluster Summary

⊿ Cluster Means

Cluster	Count	Days in Treatment	Age	Cash Collections	Insurance Collections
1	368	27.7	28.9	1155.5	14599.9
2	106	30.3	25.0	1962.4	47642.5
3	281	29.6	50.8	2047.6	29058.8
4	137	28.7	43.9	27433.2	961.4
5	248	8.4	34.0	2606.3	5345.3

Figure 8.8   Hierarchical Cluster summary.

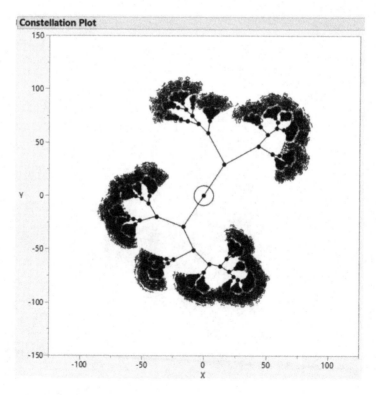

Figure 8.9   Hierarchical Clustering Constellation plot.

Stepwise regressions were performed with the dependent variable days in treatment, with independent variables: two categories of marital status, primary drug of choice, opportunity owner, insurance collections, and insurance plan. The resulting adjusted R^2 of 0.20, the significance of the F tests, and the significance of the t-tests indicated useful results but not ideal. Adding the clusters to the regression improved the ability to predict days in treatment with a new adjusted R^2 of 0.85. The lack of fit test indicates that the stepwise regression results are nonlinear. The summary output is presented in Appendix A; detailed output is available upon request from the authors.

Both clustering methods have proven valuable partitions with the data. While little significance exists in traditional demographic variables, the resulting clusters do exhibit statistical differences that contribute to a greater understanding of client treatment characteristics and successful outcomes (treatment completion). Single factor ANOVA results using clusters follow in Table 8.3.

TABLE 8.3 Significant Factor Differences for Days in Treatment Based on Clusters

Response Variable	Factor	Significant Pairs	Difference	p-value
Age	K Means Clusters	C2 versus C4	24.2 years	<0.0001
		C2 versus C1	18.3 years	<0.0001
		C3 versus C4	16.0 years	<0.0001
		C3 versus C1	10.1 years	<0.0001
		C2 versus C3	8.2 years	<0.0001
		C1 versus C4	5.9 years	<0.0001
	Hierarchical Clusters	C3 versus C2	25.9 years	<0.0001
		C3 versus C1	21.9 years	<0.0001
		C4 versus C2	18.9 years	<0.0001
		C3 versus C5	16.8 years	<0.0001
		C4 versus C1	15.0 years	<0.0001
		C4 versus C5	9.8 years	<0.0001
		C5 versus C2	9.1 years	<0.0001
		C3 versus C4	7.0 years	<0.0001
		C5 versus C1	5.2 years	<0.0001
		C1 versus C2	3.9 years	0.0028
Days in Treatment	K Means Clusters	C5 versus C1	72.9 days	<0.0001
		C5 versus C3	52.8 days	<0.0001
		C5 versus C4	52.1 days	<0.0001
		C5 versus C2	52.0 days	<0.0001

(continued)

TABLE 8.3 Significant Factor Differences for Days in Treatment Based on Clusters (continued)

Response Variable	Factor	Significant Pairs	Difference	p-value
Days in Treatment (continued)	K Means Clusters (continued)	C2 versus C1	20.9 days	<0.0001
		C4 versus C1	20.8 days	<0.0001
		C3 versus C1	20.1 days	<0.0001
	Hierarchical Clusters	C2 versus C5	21.9 days	<0.0001
		C3 versus C5	21.2 days	<0.0001
		C4 versus C5	20.3 days	<0.0001
		C1 versus C5	19.4 days	<0.0001
		C2 versus C1	2.5 days	<0.0001
		C3 versus C1	1.9 days	<0.0001
Cash Collections	K Means Clusters	C5 versus C4	$32,746	<0.0001
		C5 versus C2	$32,482	<0.0001
		C5 versus C1	$32,340	<0.0001
		C3 versus C4	$26,165	<0.0001
		C3 versus C2	$25,901	<0.0001
		C3 versus C1	$25,758	<0.0001
	Hierarchical Clusters	C4 versus C1	$26,278	<0.0001
		C4 versus C2	$25,471	<0.0001
		C4 versus C3	$25,386	<0.0001
		C4 versus C5	$24,827	<0.0001
		C5 versus C1	$1,451	0.0044
Insurance Collections	K Means Clusters	C2 versus C3	$24,104	<0.0001
		C4 versus C3	$22,890	<0.0001
		C2 versus C1	$19,958	<0.0001
		C4 versus C4	$18,754	<0.0001
		C1 versus C3	$4,146	0.0423
	Hierarchical Clusters	C2 versus C4	$46,681	<0.0001
		C2 versus C5	$42,297	<0.0001
		C2 versus C1	$33,043	<0.0001
		C3 versus C4	$28,097	<0.0001
		C3 versus C5	$23,714	<0.0001
		C2 versus C3	$18,584	<0.0001
		C3 versus C1	$14,459	<0.0001
		C1 versus C4	$13,639	<0.0001
		C1 versus C5	$9,255	<0.0001
		C5 versus C4	$4,384	0.0013

Column Contributions				
Term	Number of Splits	SS		Portion
K Means Cluster	1	82843.7404		0.7754
Discharge Type	1	14362.5737		0.1344
Hierarchical Cluster	2	4798.7601		0.0449
Cash Collections	5	2962.29406		0.0277
Gender	2	1003.43521		0.0094
Insurance Collections	2	873.796517		0.0082
Age	0	0		0.0000
BCBS Plan	0	0		0.0000
Marital Status	0	0		0.0000
Drug of Choice 1	0	0		0.0000

Figure 8.10 Partition Column Contributions.

Further examination of the variable days in treatment using partitioning produced an R^2 of 0.636 with 10 splits. Not surprisingly, the most significant factor in determining days in treatment is discharge type. Gender and insurance plan provided the next best splits, followed by age group, primary drug of choice, and marital status. Addition of the K Means clusters and hierarchical clusters yield an R^2 of .810 in 13 splits. The column contribution report in Figure 8.10 confirms the effectiveness of the clustering procedures. The small tree view is available in Appendix A. The complete analysis output is available upon request from the authors.

The addition of clusters supported an ordinal logistic fit for discharge type. The results of the stepwise logistic model identified primary drug of choice, insurance collections, days in treatment, and hierarchical clusters as significant in prediction of successful treatment completion (discharge type). Note that the inclusion of the insurance collection variable acts as a surrogate variable for the complexity of the insurance approval process. The R^2 value generated was 0.39 while the lack of fit was rejected, indicating a linear model. Summary output is provided in Appendix A; detailed output is available upon request from the authors.

Text mining was completed on the free response questions from the satisfaction surveys. Though this data could not be directly tied to the quantitative and qualitative variables, the analysis did reveal areas in which Futures is very strong, and a much smaller number of areas in which Futures should improve. Most frequent findings are presented in Table 8.4.

The alumni postdischarge survey response frequencies are provided in Figures 8.11 and 8.12. Figure 8.11 reports substance use after discharge from Futures, and Figure 8.12 reports response frequencies for questions about productivity and quality of life. In both cases, results are subject to suspected response bias. Alumni are much less likely to respond if they have engaged in continued substance use. For this reason, we cannot establish statistical significance.

TABLE 8.4 Text Mining Findings From Satisfaction Survey	
Survey Question	
Insight gained during DBT	Over 95% positive responses Mindfulness/meditation viewed very positively "Live in the moment" commonly referenced Accept/embrace/control emotions Communication is vital
Biggest challenge of DBT	Radical acceptance Focus/attention Turning negative into positive Regulating emotions Being open/honest/vulnerable
Staff to be praised	Many staff members received positive mention Top 10 staff members: number of mentions ranged from 62 down to 17
Staff to be trained	Fewer staff members received negative commentary Bottom 10 staff members: number of mentions ranged from 3 to 13
Suggestions	Improve communications between all individuals in the center More consistent enforcement of handbook Extended and more frequent outings More vegetables/salads More positive messages in meetings at start and end of day Update/improve media room More phone time Improved medication management

OUTCOMES

Producing definitive outcomes from alcohol and rehabilitation center facilities is not a simple task. Software adoption in the healthcare industry is far behind that of other industries, resulting in more difficulty in gathering and analyzing useful data. In the face of these difficulties, Futures has implemented multiple systems, aggregating extracts from each system, to develop complete data.

Goal 1: *Understand the client population and the factors that led to successful completion of a rehabilitation program.*

With the exception of the satisfaction survey, data collected reflected admissions from February 2014 to May 2016. Characterization of this data on existing data fields was only mildly illuminating. Sustained insurance coverage is a primary factor in retaining clients though, as we know, loss of insurance does not result in discharge. Insurance collection was also a

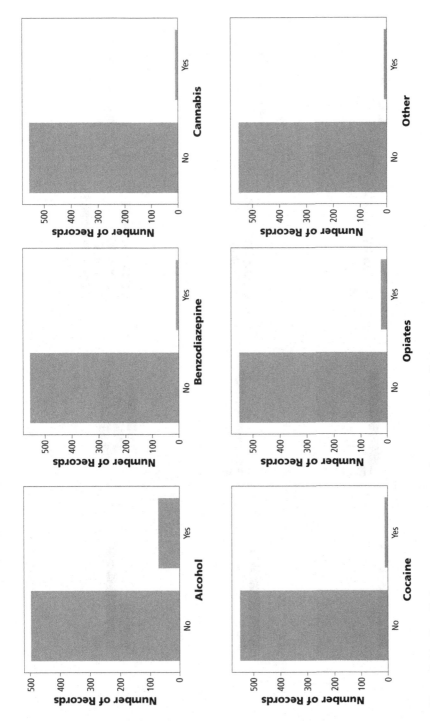

Figure 8.11 Postdischarge survey response substance use after discharge.

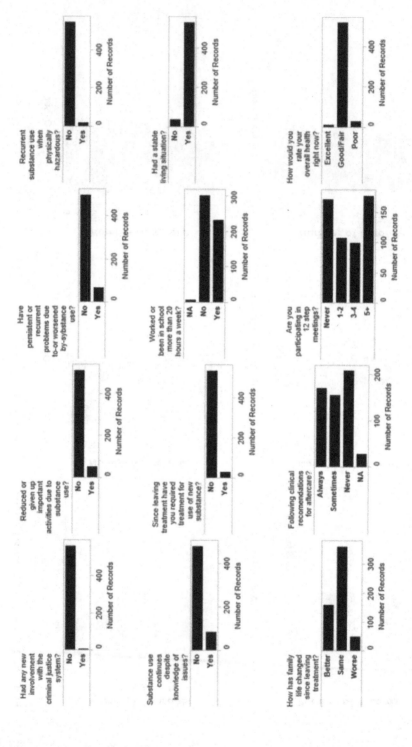

Figure 8.12 Postdischarge survey response frequency.

leading factor in the type of discharge and timing of discharge. Age group, gender, marital status and primary drug of choice factored into treatment duration, but the percentage of total variation explained (adjusted R^2) remained low at 20%.

The creation of clusters using K Means and hierarchical methods achieved the greatest impact. When these clusters were used in a decision tree on the number of days in treatment, a stepwise regression predicting the number of days in treatment, and a stepwise ordinal logistic regression to predict discharge type, the R^2 values increased substantially: exceeding 80% in all three cases. The clusters provided meaningful characterization of clients that may be applied to potential new clients in order to predict their likelihood of treatment completion and duration of stay.

Goal 2: *Understand the effectiveness of aspects of facility and treatment based on client survey responses.*

Analysis of the satisfaction survey offered good insights into the most effective elements of treatment as well as aspects of care that may be detrimental to treatment completion. Since implementing this survey 272 clients have responded. Though this is a small population, it is a more recent and therefore more relevant population when considering the implications of the responses. ANOVA found differences in the duration of treatment by several demographic factors; such as gender, some age groups, divorced versus single clients, discharge type, and the primary drug of choice.

More relevant ANOVA results were generated when analyzing the Likert scale questions. A positive experience of a new client with the medical staff within the first 48 hours could extend the duration of treatment by at least 6 days. A more positive experience with the medical administration could extend the duration of treatment by at least 3.12 days. Effective collaboration in setting treatment goals yields, at least an additional 6.85 days in treatment. Treatment by admissions staff could increase the length of stay by as many as 15.83 days. Finally, positive experiences with the RA staff could extend treatment duration up to an additional 4.60 days. Any of these extensions of treatment duration could yield significant increases in clients who reached completion of treatment, sobriety, and improved long-term quality of life.

Results of text mining highlighted areas of strength in care at Futures, while also highlighting areas that could benefit from improvement. The current individualized treatment programs garnered very positive responses. This endorsement confirmed that the facility is able to reach and engage its clients. Communication and consistency in enforcement of rules were identified as areas needing improvement.

Goal 3: *Understand the factors that lead to clients' ability to remain sober after their departure from the center.*

Analysis results were less supportive of the third goal. Response bias was a significant factor and precluded any meaningful statistical analysis.

RECOMMENDATIONS

The most valuable outcome from this research has been the identification of needs for future data collection that will allow more accurate and credible analyses to be performed. This creates a challenge for Futures in trying to implement systems that provide greater flexibility, while also keeping in mind the need to be fiscally responsible in their selection of systems. Enterprise level systems for use in health care tend to be targeted at large hospital systems; and though they may be scalable to the needs of a single rehabilitation facility, the costs can be insurmountable when considering the number of clients who are served.

Long-term outcomes were very difficult to assess in the setting. In particular, we were faced with the issue of nonresponse or potentially biased or dishonest responses from former clients. This was particularly problematic when evaluating the postdischarge surveys.

However, this does not mean that outcomes cannot be assessed. The survey has been redesigned in hopes of reducing the shame involved in answering questions and also to provide more detail and clarification in responses. Futures should continue moving forward, building trusting relationships with alumni to reduce the biases.

Examining the CDC data on crude death rates by age group across the nation over the last several years, it becomes clear that substance abuse and alcohol abuse are not a young person's game. Older Americans are just as susceptible to the diseases of alcoholism and addiction. If Futures can develop programs targeting issues uniquely tied to aging, they will be able to expand their older demographic, while simultaneously improving treatment programs and increasing sobriety in older patients. Improved communication with clients and consistent enforcement of rules are problems of a critical nature, but they can be somewhat easily addressed though training and revised procedures. Many of the client responses targeted perceived deficiencies related to inconsistent terminology or enforcement that had little to do with actual deficiencies in the treatment program. Improved communication with, and training of, staff should also take a high priority. Balancing the need for consistency while also trying to support clients as much as possible is not an easy task. Staff members take on a parental role of sorts, balancing compassion with structure and enforcement of rules.

As a substance and alcohol abuse rehabilitation center, Futures is reaching for higher goals. It seeks to not just report from its data, but too in fact analyze its data and find statistical significance to help continually improve the quality of care and its ability to successfully treat and motivate clients. All of these recommendations will propel Futures in this direction.

APPENDIX A: SELECTED ANALYSIS OUTPUTS: Stepwise Regression Summary Output

Source	LogWorth	PValue
K Means Cluster(1-3&4&2)	57.520	0.00000
Discharge Type(Medical Administrative&Other&Administrative&AMA / AMA-Treatment Completion)	54.613	0.00000
Hierarchical Cluster(5-1&4&2&3)	37.343	0.00000
Cash Collections	1.910	0.01230
Insurance Collections	1.445	0.03587

Remove Add Edit [ ] FDR

Lack Of Fit

Source	DF	Sum of Squares	Mean Square	F Ratio
Lack Of Fit	939	13869.521	14.7705	1.3135
Pure Error	194	2181.552	11.2451	Prob > F
Total Error	1133	16051.073		0.0095*
				Max RSq
				0.9800

Summary of Fit

RSquare	0.852607
RSquare Adj	0.851957
Root Mean Square Error	3.763891
Mean of Response	24.30202
Observations (or Sum Wgts)	1139

Analysis of Variance

Source	DF	Sum of Squares	Mean Square	F Ratio
Model	5	92849.03	18569.8	1310.790
Error	1133	16051.07	14.2	Prob > F
C. Total	1138	108900.11		<.0001*

Parameter Estimates

Term	Estimate	Std Error	t Ratio	Prob>|t|
Intercept	18.108723	0.190418	95.10	<.0001*
Discharge Type(Medical Administrative&Other&Administrative&AMA / ASA-Treatment Completion)	-3.088148	0.186457	-16.56	<.0001*
Cash Collections	3.264e-5	0.000013	2.51	0.0123*
Insurance Collections	1.6335e-5	7.775e-6	2.10	0.0359*
K Means Cluster(1-3&4&2)	-4.613431	0.270456	-17.06	<.0001*
Hierarchical Cluster(5-1&4&2&3)	-3.557629	0.265677	-13.39	<.0001*

Stepwise Logistic Analysis

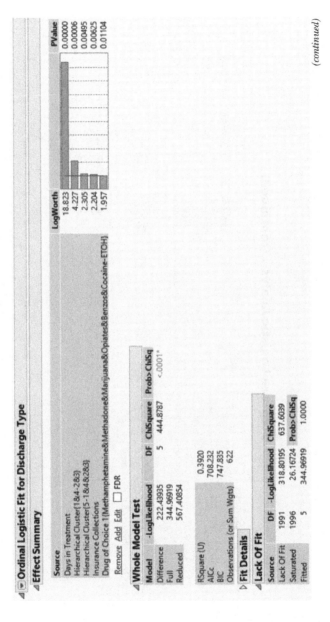

Ordinal Logistic Fit for Discharge Type

Effect Summary

Source	LogWorth	PValue
Days in Treatment	18.823	0.00000
Hierarchical Cluster{1&4-2&3}	4.227	0.00006
Hierarchical Cluster{5-1&4&2&3}	2.305	0.00495
Insurance Collections	2.204	0.00625
Drug of Choice 1{Methamphetamine&Methadone&Marijuana&Opiates&Benzos&Cocaine-ETOH}	1.957	0.01104

Remove Add Edit ☐ FDR

Whole Model Test

Model	–LogLikelihood	DF	ChiSquare	Prob>ChiSq
Difference	222.43935	5	444.8787	<.0001*
Full	344.96919			
Reduced	567.40854			

RSquare (U)	0.3920
AICc	708.232
BIC	747.835
Observations (or Sum Wgts)	622

▷ Fit Details

Lack Of Fit

Source	DF	–LogLikelihood	ChiSquare	
Lack Of Fit	1991	318.80195	637.6039	
Saturated	1996	26.16724	Prob>ChiSq	
Fitted	5	344.96919	1.0000	

(continued)

Stepwise Logistic Analysis (continued)

Parameter Estimates

Term	Estimate	Std Error	ChiSquare	Prob>ChiSq
Intercept[Administrative]	-0.700579	0.3991362	3.08	0.0792
Intercept[AMA / ASA]	2.33883401	0.4530142	26.65	<.0001*
Intercept[Medical Administrative]	2.59888016	0.4568533	32.36	<.0001*
Intercept[Other]	2.66449965	0.4577816	33.88	<.0001*
Drug of Choice 1[Methamphetamine&Methadone&Marijuana&Opiates&Benzos&Cocaine-ETOH]	0.29903449	0.1181644	6.40	0.0114*
Insurance Collections	2.97617e-5	1.0876e-5	7.49	0.0062*
Days in Treatment	-0.17282068	0.0203736	71.96	<.0001*
Hierarchical Cluster[5-1&4&2&3]	0.70558519	0.2509969	7.90	0.0049*
Hierarchical Cluster[1&4-2&3]	0.89864105	0.2396624	14.06	0.0002*

Effect Likelihood Ratio Tests

Source	Nparm	DF	L-R ChiSquare	Prob>ChiSq
Drug of Choice 1[Methamphetamine&Methadone&Marijuana&Opiates&Benzos&Cocaine-ETOH]	1	1	6.4583742	0.0110*
Insurance Collections	1	1	7.47663311	0.0063*
Days in Treatment	1	1	81.8012794	<.0001*
Hierarchical Cluster[5-1&4&2&3]	1	1	7.89773418	0.0049*
Hierarchical Cluster[1&4-2&3]	1	1	16.1263596	<.0001*

Days in Treatment Partition Results

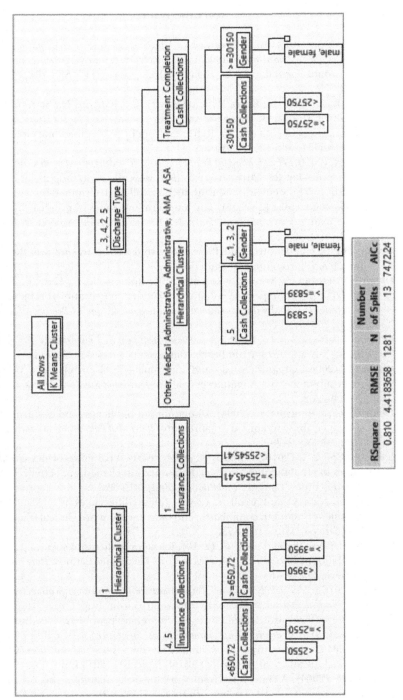

REFERENCES

Ali, M., & Mutter, R. (2016). *Patients who are privately insured receive limited follow-up services after opioid-related hospitalizations.* Retrieved June 6, 2016, from http://www.samhsa.gov/data/sites/default/files/report_2117/ShortReport-2117.html

Benishek, L., Dugosh, K., Kirby, K., Matejkowski, J., Clements, N., Seymour, B., & Festinger, D. (2014). *Prize-based contingency management for the treatment of substance abusers: A meta-analysis.* Retrieved from http://onlinelibrary.wiley.com/doi/10.1111/add.12589/abstract

Bithoney, W. (2016). *How behavioral health income will be determined by clinical outcomes* Retrieved May 25, 2016, from https://www.bdo.com/insights/industries/healthcare/how-behavioral-health-income-will-be-determined-by

Bovasso, G., & Cacciola, J., (2003). The long-term outcomes of drug use by methadone maintenance patients. *Journal of Behavioral Health Services & Research, 30*(3), 290–303.

Centers for Disease Control and Prevention. (n.d.). *CDC wonder data.* Retrieved June 6 & 17, from http://wonder.cdc.gov/

Drebing, C. Ormer, A. Krebs, C., Rosenheck, R., Rounsaville, B., Herz, L., & Penk, W. (2005). The impact of enhanced incentives on vocational rehabilitation outcomes for dually diagnosed veterans. *Journal of Applied Behavioral Analysis, 38*(3), 359–372.

Futures of Palm Beach. (n.d.). *Evidenced-based treatment and research.* Retrieved from https://www.futuresofpalmbeach.com/evidence-based-treatment/

Ghose, T. (2008) Organizational—and individual—level correlates of posttreatment substance use: A multilevel analysis. *Journal of Substance Abuse Treatment 34*, 249–262.

Heinrich, C., & Fournier, E. (2004). Dimensions of publicness and performance in substance abuse treatment organizations. *Journal of Policy Analysis and Management, 23*(1), 49–70.

Jesus, T., & Silva, I. (2016). Towards an evidence-based patient-provider communication in rehabilitation: linking communication elements to better rehabilitation outcomes. *Clinical Rehabilitation, 30*(4), 315–328.

Milligan, C., Nich, C., & Carroll, K. (2004). Ethnic differences in substance abuse treatment retention, compliance, and outcome from two clinical trials. *Psychiatric Services, 55*(2), 167–173.

Nielson, A., Bonn, S., & Wilson, G. (2010). Racial prejudice and spending on drug rehabilitation: The role of attitudes towards Blacks and Latinos. *Race and Social Problems, 2*, 149–163.

PRWeb. (2016). *U.S. rehab now providing immediate insurance verification for Florida drug and alcohol rehab centers.* Retrieved 2016 from http://www.prweb.com/releases/florida-drug-rehab/drug-alcohol-rehab/prweb13234307.htm

SAMHSHA. (2014). *A day in the life of young adults: Substance use facts.* Retrieved June 6, 2016, from http://www.samhsa.gov/data/sites/default/files/CBHSQ-SR168-TypicalDay-2014/CBHSQ-SR168-TypicalDay-2014.htm

Simpson, D. (2004). A conceptual framework for drug treatment process and outcome. *Journal of Substance Abuse Treatment, 27*, 99–121.

Yih-Ing, H., Yu-Chuang, H., Teruya, C., & Anglin, M. (2004, Spring). Gender differences in treatment outcomes over a three-year period: A path model analysis. *The Journal of Drug Issues, 32*(2), 419–439.

CHAPTER 9

AN EXTENDED H-INDEX

A New Method to Evaluate Scientists' Impact

Feng Yang and Xiya Zu
University of Science and Technology of China

Zhimin Huang[1]
Adelphi University and Beijing Institute of Technology

ABSTRACT

Researcher evaluation is increasingly popular and important in the scientific community. Measures to assess the scientific impact of a researcher have been proposed through lots of scientists' efforts. Among various methods, the *h*-index is the most widely used, in that it incorporates the quantity and quality of a scientist's productivity, and it can be conveniently used. Nevertheless, there are some drawbacks to using the *h*-index. In order to remedy some disadvantages of the *h*-index, scientists have proposed some *h*-type indices. However, few indicators take account of the quality of citations of a paper. Most indices treat all citations equally. But the citation quality should be a key factor in the evaluation result. A paper must be valuably cited by a high quality paper, but it does not illustrate its value cited by marginal articles. We then propose a

Contemporary Perspectives on Data Mining, Volume 3, pages 135–145
Copyright © 2018 by Information Age Publishing
All rights of reproduction in any form reserved.

new index, the extended h-index (EHI), which considers the role of citation quality in evaluating a researcher's impact. We analyze the difference between the EHI and other four h-type indices, and explore their relationships using Spearman correlation analysis and factor analysis. The results show that the EHI can effectively evaluate the impact of a researcher. The EHI provides a new way of thinking that any h-type indicators can apply; that is, regarding the number of the high quality citation as an important criterion to measure the quality of a paper, and then evaluate the impact of a researcher.

Evaluation of the excellence of a scientist is one of the most important tasks for human beings. Evaluation results have a great influence on the progress of human society, which is closely related to the enthusiasm of scientists and the atmosphere of scientific research. Assessing the individual performance of scientists or scientific works reasonably and fairly is a common concern in the scientific community. The evaluation result of a scientist can provide an important basis for him seeking promotion, career advancement, and selective funding and rewards (Abramo, D'Angelo, & Viel, 2013). Objective evaluation is of great significance for stimulating the innovative potential of researchers and promoting the scientific research.

Data mining plays an important role in evaluation of a researcher. Frawley, Piatetsky-Shapiro, and Matheus (1992) defined data mining as a process of nontrivial extraction of implicit, previously unknown, and potentially useful information from data in databases. Modern science has developed for hundreds of years generating large number and redundancy data, from which we can dig out useful information to evaluate the excellence of a researcher. The evaluation of an individual's impact is an important application of data mining.

Peer review is a type of direct evaluation of individual academic achievement and scientific research achievement. It is effective but not easy to be widely used. Because reviewers should carefully review the paper in peer review, more time and energy is used. Compared to peer review, bibliometrics achieve the rationality of time and costs (Abramo et al., 2013). Among the many indicators, the single criteria—such as the measure just considering the number of articles published by the author, without caring about the quality of the papers—cannot accurately reflect the impact of a scientist. So, the h-index that considers both quantity and quality has attracted wide attention since it was proposed by Hirsch in 2005 (Ball, 2005; Bornmann & Daniel, 2005; Glänzel & Persson, 2005; Bar-Ilan, 2006; Cronin & Meho, 2006; Liang, 2006), and it has become one of the most popular indicators to measure a researcher's lifetime achievement.

The h-index is defined as: "A scientist has index h if h of his or her Np papers have at least h citations each and the other (Np–h) papers have $\leq h$ citations each" (Hirsch, 2005, p. 16569). It means the first h publications receive at least h citations, each ranked in decreasing order of the number of citations of each paper, and the h is the maximum number. These h papers form h-core (Rousseau, 2006). There are some advantages and disadvantages of the h-index we can find in literature. It is a very simple index that can be applied to any level of objects and closely correlated to total publications; and it discourages unimportant work, because papers that have no or few citations do not influence its value. Of course criticism is inevitable: the h-index is insensitive to excellent highly cited papers and detrimental to the newcomers; it has a low degree of discrimination, and can never decrease; and it doesn't take into account the number of coauthors and their respective contribution to a paper (Hirsch, 2005; Glänzel, 2006; Jin, Liang, & Rousseau, 2007).

For the virtues and drawbacks of the h-index, scientists have proposed some variants to evaluate individual achievement more scientifically. Egghe (2006a, 2006b) proposed g-index, defined as the highest number g of publications that together received g^2 or more citations. G-index is the first h-type index, it breaks the limit of the total amount of the papers and is more favorable to those researchers who have less output with highly cited (Zhou, 2011). The Kosmulski (2006) $h(2)$-index is $h(2)$ if the first $h(2)$ publications, ranked in decreasing order of the number of citations, received at least $h^2(2)$ citations each. The $h(2)$-index is similar to the g-index, it also gives more weight to high cited papers. The a-index introduced by Jin (2006) is the average of citations the articles in the h-core received. The a-index is sensitive to more widely cited papers in h-core. Jin et al. (2007) proposed the R-index and AR-index. The R-index is the square root of the total number of citations of papers in the h-core; it improves the sensitivity and discriminability of the papers in the h-core. The AR-index is a modification of the R-index, which takes the age of the publications as a determinant. Järvelin and Persson (2008) proposed a discounted cumulated impact (DCI) index, which is based on the idea of devaluing old citations and incorporating both time and weight of citations. The w-index proposed by Wu (2010) is defined as: If a researcher's w papers have received at least $10w$ citations each, and other papers have fewer than $10(w + 1)$ citations each, the researcher's w-index is w. The w-index pays more attention to highly cited papers and accurately reflects the influence of a researcher's top publications. There are some other alternatives introduced that may overcome some disadvantages of the h-index, such as the b-index (Bornmann & Mutz, 2007), hw index (Egghe & Rousseau, 2008), e-index (Zhang, 2009), and $\hbar$ index (Hirsch, 2010).

Although there are various indicators, all indices except DCI ignore the quality of citations. These indicators view all citations as equally important: just consider the number of citations received by each paper, and do not care about the quality of these citations. However, the quality of citations each paper receives is undoubtedly a decisive factor in the evaluation of an individual's impact. To illustrate, assume a researcher published 80 papers, which were cited 100 times each by high quality articles; another researcher also has 80 papers, which received 100 citations each by marginal papers. Can we say the two scientists have the same achievement? Obviously, we cannot say that.

The methods that do not consider the quality of citations are not accurate enough to evaluate those who have high quality papers but receive fewer citations. This phenomenon may result from the following: First, the paper's point of focus is so advanced that many scholars have not yet involved this knowledge; and second, the content is too complicated and profound to understand, so ordinary scholars cannot deeply study the paper. In addition, an author's popularity also affects the citation rate of the paper. Unfamous researchers' papers have low display degree and are infrequently cited. However, these situations should not be reasons to deny a paper's value.

We can see that not every citation reflects the impact of an article, only the citations with high quality truly illustrate a paper's value. Based on this, this paper proposes a new measure—the extended h-index (EHI)—as an objective way to evaluate a researcher's output, especially regarding excellent papers.

THE EXTENDED h-INDEX

We define the EHI as follows: If a scientist has n papers, each paper has at least $2n$ citations and n of them are published in top journals, n is the maximum number, then the researcher's EHI is n. Top journals refer to journals belonging to the first division according to the divisions of SCI (Science Citation Index) journal grades. Top journals have higher authority in the field, are the periodicals that scholars often read, and the journals that people consider when they contribute a paper (Jin, Wang, & Ren, 2000). Papers included in top journals have to go through rigorous review, so the quality of publications is guaranteed. We call the citing papers published in top journals top citations. The EHI takes into consideration the widely cited papers and the quality of citing publications, it can effectively evaluate a researcher's impact.

There are noticeable differences between the EHI and the h-index, because the EHI focus on the papers that have great impact in the field. In the next section, we compare the ranks of 10 economists ranked by the EHI and four other indicators, and present analysis of the results. In the last section, we summarize the application and shortcomings of the EHI, discuss its further improvement, and give some advice on the evaluative system.

COMPARISON OF THE EHI WITH OTHER METHODS

We made a comparison of the EHI and four other indicators—h-index, g-index, w-index and a-index—using the evaluation results of 10 economists to test the effectiveness of the EHI. We chose 10 economists ranked in the top 10% of the RePEc database, and counted the number of publications, the number of citations each paper received, and the number of top citations of each paper. The original data were collected in April 2016 from the Web of Science (WoS) and the Journal Citation Report (JCR) provided by Thomson.

Table 9.1 shows the evaluation results of the EHI and other indices. To respect the privacy of these scientists, we used their initials to represent them. We first analyzed the results of the 10 economists judged by the EHI and the h-index. As the table reveals, we note that STJ and LZ have no difference in h-index, but LZ is ranked 3rd and STJ is ranked 5th according to the EHI, it means LZ has more masterworks than STJ, even their h-index is the same. The h-index puts JP and PEC at the 6th and 7th place, yet their EHIs are the same: both rank 8th. KJH is ranked 4th by the h-index, better than most of the economists, but via the EHI, KJH is just ranked 7th. NWK is contrary to the situation of KJH. Furthermore, JP is better than NWK assessed by h-index, while NWK is more excellent than JP by the EHI. Similarly, STJ's $h = 25$, larger than NWK's $h = 18$, yet STJ's EHI = 16 is smaller than NWK's EHI = 17. KJH's $h = 22$ is larger than RKS's $h = 20$, however RKS is better than KJH assessed by the EHI. PEC and NWK have the same $h = 18$, whereas their EHI are 13 and 17 respectively.

We can see that the EHI is very different from the h-index, because the EHI is more concerned about the papers that have great impact in the field.

TABLE 9.1	Evaluation of the 10 Economists									
	EHI		h-index		g-index		w-index		a-index	
Name	Value	Rank	Value	Rank	Value	Rank	Value	Rank	Value	Rank
STJ	16	5	25	3	48	4	8	3	84.56	8
LZ	20	3	25	3	68	1	12	1	177	2
RCM	12	9	17	8	26	10	9	2	135.71	4
JP	13	8	19	6	33	9	5	5	50.11	9
PEC	13	8	18	7	37	6	7	4	165.06	3
BT	21	2	27	2	53	2	9	2	96.63	7
IGW	24	1	29	1	50	3	12	1	212.07	1
KJH	14	7	22	4	35	7	5	5	49.68	10
RKS	15	6	20	5	46	5	9	2	105.55	6
NWK	17	4	18	7	34	8	9	2	109.83	5

We further analyzed the differences among all methods. We first looked at IGW, he is evaluated as the best scientist among the 10 economists by the EHI, h-index, w-index, and a-index; but he is ranked 3rd in the g-index. BT ranks 2nd through the EHI, h-index, g-index, and w-index; but by the a-index, he is ranked just 7th, which is clearly too low. STJ has similar results according to the EHI, h-index, g-index, and w-index; via the a-index he ranks in the middle or upper position, but in 8th place. LZ is at 1st, 2nd, or 3rd place by all methods, his ranks are not very different. The EHI, h-index, g-index, and a-index put RKS at 6th, 5th, 5th, 6th places respectively, which are very close; but at 2nd place via the w-index this scientist is obviously higher. KJH is ranked higher by the h-index and is the worst by the a-index. PEC is ranked 8th, 7th, and 6th according to the EHI, h-index, and g-index; but by the w-index and a-index, he ranks 4th and 3rd. The EHI, g-index, and a-index respectively put JP at 8th, 9th, and 9th places; but he ranks slightly higher through the h-index and w-index. The last scientist, RCM, is ranked 9th, 8th, and 10th (bottom position) by the EHI, h-index and g-index; but the w-index and a-index put RCM at 2nd and 4th places, which are front positions.

We observe that the evaluation results are very different through the five measures. But we can obviously notice that the ranking of an individual by the EHI is always consistent with the evaluation results of most indicators. It shows that the EHI has good stability and can accurately evaluate the excellence of a scientist.

To visualize the relationship among the five measures, we compute Spearman's ranking correlation coefficient. The results are presented in Table 9.2.

The highest correlation is found between the h-index and the g-index (0.837); the h-index is also high correlated with the EHI. Correlation coefficients between other indices are not high.

Bornmann, Mutz, and Daniel (2008) used an exploratory factor analysis to investigate basic dimensions that indicate how the nine h-type indicators calculated for the B.I.F. applicants cluster. In this paper, we tried to find representative factors that indicated how the five methods evaluated the 10 economists by using exploratory factor analysis. The results are shown in Tables 9.3, 9.4, and 9.5.

TABLE 9.2	Correlation Coefficients Among Five Methods				
Rank	EHI	h-index	g-index	w-index	a-index
EHI	1.000				
h-index	0.806	1.000			
g-index	0.794	0.837	1.000		
w-index	0.673	0.339	0.528	1.000	
a-index	0.367	0.062	0.333	0.724	1.000

TABLE 9.3	Total Variance Explained					
	Initial Eigenvalues			Extraction Sums of Squared Loadings		
Component	Total	% of Variance	Cumulative %	Total	% of Variance	Cumulative %
EHI	3.25	64.992	64.992	3.25	64.992	64.992
h-index	1.24	24.8	89.792	1.24	24.8	89.792
g-index	0.278	5.555	95.346			
w-index	0.147	2.948	98.294			
a-index	0.085	1.706	100			

TABLE 9.4	Communalities	
	Initial	Extraction
EHI	1.000	0.891
h-index	1.000	0.946
g-index	1.000	0.874
w-index	1.000	0.878
a-index	1.000	0.901

TABLE 9.5	Component Matrix	
	Factor 1	Factor 2
EHI	0.931	−0.156
h-index	0.801	−0.551
g-index	0.895	−0.269
w-index	0.790	0.503
a-index	0.561	0.766

Table 9.3 shows that the cumulative contribution rate of the first two factors with eigenvalues larger than 1 is 89.792%, which indicates that 89.792% of the total variance can be explained by the two latent factors, of which Factor 1 explained 64.992%, and Factor 2 explained 24.800%. We can see from Table 9.4, the communality of each variable (index) is greater than 0.8, and most of them are close to or higher than 0.9; this suggests the two factors can well reflect the most information of the original variables. Table 9.5 shows the component matrix for the extracted two factors and the five indices. It clearly shows that the factor loadings of all variables on Factor 1 are high, and the a-index loads highest on Factor 2. Based on this, we refer to Factor 1 as "quality of the output" and to Factor 2 as "quantity of the output." In all indices, the EHI loads the highest on Factor 1 with

coefficient of 0.931. This result shows that the EHI has the highest correlation with the quality of the output.

DISCUSSIONS

Due to the advantages and disadvantages of the h-index, various h-type indices have been proposed to supplement it. However, no indicator considers the quality of citations of a paper, which is a determinant to the quality of the paper, and the quality of papers is the most important criterion for evaluating an individual's scientific research output; thus, citation quality must be an important factor that influences the evaluation result. We propose the EHI to fill the gap of the evaluation system. The EHI is actually an improvement on the h-index, as it incorporates the number of citations and top citations each paper has received; these two yardsticks are well able to quantify the quality of a paper. Scientific excellence is usually expressed in a scientist's best publications (Fröhlich, 2001), so a good measure must accurately reflect a researcher's most representative output.

Like the h-index, the EHI can also be used for the evaluation of journals (Braun, Glänzel, & Schubert, 2005), topics (Banks, 2006; STIMULATE6 Group, 2007), conference (Sidiropoulos, Katsaros, & Manolopoulos, 2007), scientific institutions (Molinari & Molinari, 2008), even library loans per category (Liu & Rousseau, 2007), and other objects.

There are some problems with the EHI, such as it is difficult to rank those who have the same index by using only one index. We can use the combination of the EHI and the a-index to compensate for the insufficiency of a single index. The EHI (with the highest loading on Factor 1 in factor analysis) relates to the quality of a researcher's output, and the a-index (with the highest loading on Factor 2 in factor analysis) relates to the quantity of a researcher's papers.

The EHI inevitably exists with some disadvantages like other indexes using citation analysis (Kosmulski, 2006; Jin et al., 2007), that is:

- It has field dependency.
- The index may be improved by self-citations or mutual citations.
- The achievement of scientists of different ages cannot be compared.
- It is hard to collect all data for calculating the index from various databases.

Although the EHI requires more data than the h-index, it is easy to collect what one needs from the WoS. If WoS would provide the number of citing articles published in top journals that each paper received, the EHI could be as convenient to use as the h-index.

The EHI provides a new thinking about the evaluation system; that is, the quality of citing journals has a significant impact on the achievement of a scientist, which can be used in any index that uses citation analysis. We take the g-index as an example: Ranking one's articles in decreasing order of the number of top citations, we define the new index is g if the highest number g of papers together has at least g^2 top citations.

For future research, one can make further studies to improve the EHI for assessing an individual's scientific achievement more accurately. We propose three possible variants: (a) It makes a difference to consider the level of the authors of the citing publications in its evaluation. Outstanding scientists play an important role in the spread of the cited paper, allowing more people to notice and study it. So it is suitable to take the average EHI of the authors into consideration; (b) In addition, the EHI pays more attention to a scientist's representative output. We can further give different weights to different grades of journals to evaluate a more comprehensive influence of a research. According to Pinski and Narin (1976), the weight of a prestigious journal should be higher than the peripheral one; and (c) It is not reasonable to use a fixed index to compare scientists in different fields, because different disciplines have their own characteristic in the aspects of research scale, research methods and citation behavior. These characteristics determine the difference in the overall level of citation frequency of each subject (Jin, Wang, & Ren, 2000). Different coefficients of the number of citations and the number of top citations each paper received in different fields can be used to overcome the field dependency.

ACKNOWLEDGMENTS

The authors would like to thank the National Natural Science Foundation of China (Grant Nos. 71322101, 71271195, 71110107024) for their financial support.

NOTE

1. Professor Zhimin Huang is the corresponding author for this chapter. Email: huang@adelphi.edu

REFERENCES

Abramo G., D'Angelo, C., & Viel, F. (2013). Assessing the accuracy of the h- and g-indices for measuring researchers' productivity. *Journal of the American Society for Information Science and Technology, 64*(6), 1224–1234.

Ball P. (2005). Index aims for fair ranking of scientists. *Nature, 436*(7053), 900.

Banks M. G. (2006). An extension of the Hirsch index: Indexing scientific topics and compounds. *Scientometrics, 69*(1), 161–168.

Bar-Ilan J. (2006). H-index for Price medalists revisited. *ISSI Newsletter, 2*(1), 3–5.

Bornmann L., & Daniel. H. (2005). Does the *h*-index for ranking of scientists really work? *Scientometrics, 65*(3), 391–392.

Bornmann L., Mutz, R., & Daniel, H. (2007). The *b*-index as a measure of scientific excellence. *International Journal of Scientometrics, Informetrics and Bibliometrics, 11*(1).

Bornmann L., Mutz R., & Daniel, H. (2009). Are there better indices for evaluation purposes than the h-index? A comparison of nine different variants of the *h*-index using data from biomedicine. *Journal of the American Society for Information Science and Technology, 59*(5), 830–837.

Braun, T., Glänzel, W., & Schubert, A. (2005). A Hirsch-type index for journals. *The Scientist, 19*(22), 8.

Cronin, B., & Meho, L. (2006). Using the *h*-index to rank influential information scientists. *Journal of the American Society for Information Science and Technology, 57*(9), 1275–1278.

Egghe, L. (2006a). An improvement of the *h*-index: The *g*-index. *ISSI newsletter, 2*(1), 8–9.

Egghe, L. (2006b). Theory and practice of the *g*-index. *Scientometrics, 69*(1), 131–152.

Egghe, L., & Rousseau, R. (2008). An *h*-index weighted by citation impact. *Information Processing & Management, 44*(2), 770–780.

Frawley, W., Piatetsky-Shapiro, G., & Matheus, C. (1992). Knowledge discovery in databases: An overview, *AI Magazine 13*(3), 57–70.

Fröhlich, H. (2001). It all depends on the individuals. Research promotion: A balanced system of control. *BIF Futura, 16*(2), 69–77.

Glänzel, W. (2006). On the opportunities and limitations of the *h*-index. *Science Focus, 1*(1), 10–11 (in Chinese).

Glänzel, W., & Persson, O. (2005). *H*-index for Price medalists. *ISSI newsletter, 1*(4), 15–18.

Hirsch, J. E. (2005). An index to quantify an individual's scientific research output. *Proceedings of the National Academy of Sciences of the United States of America, 102*(46), 16569–16572.

Hirsch, J. E. (2010). An index to quantify an individual's scientific research output that takes into account the effect of multiple coauthorship. *Scientometrics, 85*(3), 741–754.

Järvelin, K., & Persson, O. (2008). The DCI index: Discounted cumulated impact-based research evaluation. *Journal of the American Society for Information Science and Technology, 59*(9), 1433–1440.

Jin, B. (2006). *H*-index: An evaluation indicator proposed by scientist. *Science Focus, 1*(1), 8–9.

Jin, B., Liang, L., & Rousseau, R. (2007). The *R*- and *AR*-indices: Complementing the *h*-index. *Chinese Science Bulletin, 52*(6), 855–863.

Jin, B., Wang, S., & Ren, S. (2000). The relationship between journal impact factors and academic quality of papers. *Chinese Journal of Scientific and Technical Periodicals, 11*(4), 202–205.

Kosmulski, M. (2006). A new Hirsch-type index saves time and works equally well as the original *h*-index. *ISSI Newsletter, 2*(3), 4–6.

Liang, L. (2006). *H*-index sequence and *h*-index matrix: Constructions and applications. *Scientometrics, 69*(1), 153–159.

Liu, Y., & Rousseau, R. (2007). Hirsch-type indices and library management: The case of Tongji University Library. *Proceedings of ISSI, 11*, 514–522.

Molinari, A., & Molinari, J. (2008). Mathematical aspects of a new criterion for ranking scientific institutions based on the *h*-index. *Scientometrics, 75*(2), 339–356.

Pinski, G., & Narin, F. (1976). Citation influence for journal aggregates of scientific publications: Theory, with application to the literature of physics. *Information Processing & Management, 12*(5), 297–312.

Rousseau, R. (2006). *New developments related to the Hirsch index.* Retrieved from http://eprints.rclis.org/7616/1/Hirsch_new_developments.pdf

Sidiropoulos, A., Katsaros, D., & Manolopoulos, Y. (2007). Generalized Hirsch *h*-index for disclosing latent facts in citation networks. *Scientometrics, 72*(2), 253–280.

Stimulate 6 Group. (2006). The Hirsch index applied to topics of interest to developing countries. *First Monday, 12*(2).

Wu, Q. (2010). The *w*-index: A measure to assess scientific impact by focusing on widely cited papers. *Journal of the American Society for Information Science and Technology, 61*(3), 609–614.

Zhang, C. T. (2009). The *e*-index, complementing the *h*-index for excess citations. *PLoS One, 4*(5), e5429.

Zhou, C. (2011). New thought for academic evaluation: Improvement, application and development of *h*-index. *China Science & Technology Resources Review, 3*, 456.

CHAPTER 10

WHY WE NEED ANALYTICS GRAND ROUNDS

Ronald Klimberg
Saint Joseph's University

Richard Pollack
Advanced Analytic Solutions

Richard Herschel
Saint Joseph's University

ABSTRACT

The number of analytics academic programs and the use of analytics by industry have been rapidly growing over the past two decades. Industry is facing a significant amount of analytics lost opportunities due to the insufficient emphasis on developing and improving problem-solving skills in the education of analytics professionals. In this paper, we propose changes to analytics academic programs that will help improve students' problem-solving skills. The focus of these changes will be on implementing relevant problem-solving/diagnosis concepts taught to physicians in their training, including the use of analytics heuristics for problem solving and an analytics grand rounds course.

Contemporary Perspectives on Data Mining, Volume 3, pages 147–159
Copyright © 2018 by Information Age Publishing

The field of analytics (or business analytics [BA] or business intelligence [BI]) has been growing exponentially in industry and academia since about the year 2000. Information systems/information technology (IS/IT) spending is taking a larger portion of an organization's budget as it has increasingly embraced analytics as a means for obtaining a competitive advantage. "Data is now relevant for leaders across every sector, and consumers of products and service stand to benefit from its application" (Manyika et al., 2011). Further, as President Obama demonstrated in his two presidential elections (and what we experienced in the 2016 U.S. presidential election), employing analytics to microtarget individuals is a critical factor in helping a candidate win an election.

What is a major cause of this analytics explosion, what has changed, and why now? The answer is Big Data. Big Data is the confluence of what is known as the 3Vs: data volume, data velocity, and data variety. Each of the 3Vs has been increasing at an exponential rate. What used to take years or months can now be done almost instantaneously. Most organizations have or are only just beginning to realize the importance of utilizing analytics.

A remarkable number of opportunities to use analytical tools and to build analytics models are now and will become possible. However, there is a significant shortage of analytically skilled individuals when at the same time demand for their talents is increasing: there is a demand for 140,000 to 190,000 people with deep analytical skills and there is a need for 1.5 million managers of BA, (Manyika et al., 2011). Demand for people who have the knowledge to use new and current technologies and software, such as Tableau, Qlik, SAS Enterprise Miner, IBM SPSS Modeler, IBM SPSS, SAS, R, S, Pig, and MapReduce is rapidly increasing. A survey conducted by *Money* magazine to identify the top skills employers put value on, included SAS, Data Mining/Data Warehousing and Data Modeling (Renzulli, Weisser, & Leonhardt, 2016). McKinsey's research "suggests that we are on the cusp of a tremendous wave of innovation, productivity, and growth, as well as new modes of competition and value capture—all driven by big data as consumers, companies, and economic sector exploit its potential" (Manyika et al., 2011). The realization that analytics should be an essential competitive competency will require a significant cultural change, as well as redefinition of numerous roles and positions in many organizations.

Academia has responded to this analytics revolution with the introduction of new analytics courses and programs. In our 2014 paper, we found 32 institutions with analytics programs (Gorman & Klimberg, 2014). Of these 32 institutions, 21 had master's programs, primarily offered by their business schools. In 2016, a search found a website on master's programs in business analytics (Master's, 2016). It listed 145 business analytics master's programs of which 29 were online and 16 were offered in a business school. This reflects a rapid increase in analytics programs within just 2 years.

One of the main objectives of this paper is to warn organizations, as well as academia, of the significant analytics opportunity lost due to this widespread proliferation of analytics. James M. Connolly in his August 3, 2016, blog post entitled "Take Analytics Education Beyond the Tools" stated that education "cannot be in just the use of the tools," but it "needs to start with what the tools can do to improve the business" (Connolly, 2016). We are educating students with the knowledge of advanced techniques and tools, but we are not providing them with sound problem-solving skills. As a result, organizations have analytics graduates armed with the latest analytics techniques and tools, yet who lack strong problem-solving skills. A primary cause of their poor problem-solving skills is that students know neither when nor where to use the techniques and tools they have learned (Powell, 2001; Grossman, 2002).

This lack of developing strong student problem-solving skills is not new to academia or to industry. Missed opportunities have been occurring for a long time. Why is it so critical now? Previously, before the turn of the 21st century and the analytics explosion, the number of analytic professionals and the number of projects were not substantial. The use of analytics was not widespread in organizations; therefore, the number of analytics projects/opportunities was relatively small. As a result, the number of lost opportunities was insignificant. Since then, the use of analytics has rapidly become more and more of an essential organizational competency. Consequently, there are substantially more actual and potential analytics projects; as a result, a considerably larger number of opportunities are being lost.

In the following section we define analytics. Then we examine the present industry landscape and its use of analytics. Next, we discuss academic analytics programs and their poor development of students' problem-solving skills. In the ensuing section, we recommend what analytics programs should add to their primary focus of teaching students problem-solving skills, similar to the way physicians are educated. In particular, we suggest adding the development of analytics heuristics as well as an analytics grand rounds (AGR) process to ensure continuous learning with the use and application of analytics.

WHAT IS ANALYTICS

What is analytics? The answer seems to depend heavily on your background. Generally speaking, if your background is in IT, you view analytics mostly as providing reports and dashboards; if your background is in statistics, you view analytics mostly as providing predictive models; and finally, if your background is in operations research/management science (OR/MS), you view analytics mostly as building simulation and optimization models.

The Institute for Operations Research and the Management Sciences (INFORMS), the largest professional society in the world for professionals in the field of operations research (OR), management science (MS), and analytics, decomposes analytics into three levels (INFORMS, 2013):

- Descriptive analytics
  - Prepares and analyzes *historical* data
  - Identifies patterns from samples for reporting of trends
- Predictive analytics
  - Predicts *future* probabilities and trends
  - Finds relationships in data that may not be readily apparent with descriptive analysis
- Prescriptive analytics
  - Evaluates and determines *new* ways to operate
  - Targets business objectives
  - Balances all constraints

Regardless of your background and the differing definitions of analytics, they all include varying degrees of emphasis on these three components: information systems (IT), statistics, and quantitative methods or operations research (OR). Further, irrespective of the level of analytics or whatever definition you may use, a general definition of analytics is that it is the process of transforming data into information to gain insight into making more informed and usually better decisions.

Typically, an organization's first venture into analytics is creating descriptive analytics. Descriptive analytics provides summary reports, queries data; it slices and dices the data, and generates charts, graphs, tables, and dashboards. Having this descriptive analytics foundation is normally a necessity to move to the next two levels: analytics of predictive and prescriptive. Predictive and prescriptive analytics includes statistical forecasting, data mining, simulation, and optimization modeling.

While the field of analytics does embrace all three levels of analytics, our focus in this paper is on the predictive and prescriptive levels of analytics. And in particular, what we consider to be the opportunity lost in these two areas of analytics in industry. Opportunity lost consists of two aspects: the misuse of analytics and the opportunities not realized.

Industry

Industry has always suffered from confusing tools with problem-solving and critical thinking. This is nothing new. But in our fast-paced, device-driven, and information-overloaded world this issue is more serious than it has ever been. There are presently more software tools, apps, and devices than at any other time in history, and the number is growing at an exponential rate.

Three areas that have contributed to confusing tools with solutions are Big Data, machine learning, and the dizzying array of software programs, both within and beyond these environments.

Big Data is one of newest buzzwords in just about any setting where copious amounts of data are available. Enormous amounts of data offer many advantages and hold great promise, some of which have already been realized. Marching to this drum beat, however, has spawned and popularized misguided concepts. One of the largest and serious misconceptions is that with Big Data, theory is not necessary. Chris Anderson (2008) has even gone further, stating that massive data makes the scientific method obsolete. Somehow, in a pure and immaculate way, data are going to explain themselves.

Nate Silver (2012) underscores how this notion in deeply misguided and flawed. With theory, strategy, and the deeper thinking that characterizes problem solving, inferences drawn from data have far greater meaning, utility, and application. "The numbers of have no way of speaking for themselves" (Silver, 2012). Sadly, this theoryless notion has not been put to rest, and the popularity and proliferation of Big Data tools, whether intended or not, are keeping deeper thinking in the backseat and immaculate statistical conception driving the car in a ditch.

Hadoop, Pig, Hive, and Spark, to name a few, have great power and utility in the Big Data world. SAS and IBM SPSS (both of which predate these tools) are used with Big Data as well, and have more widespread influence across business and academia due to their long history and deep market penetration. Open-source R is clearly a major player now as well. All of these tool sets suffer from the ill-advised notion that "findings" are going to miraculously surface once the "right technique" is applied. Currently, this view is more prevalent with Big Data apps. Moreover, in large business entities it is not uncommon to observe theoryless Big Data thinking surfacing in the use of the more classic statistical packages, such as SAS and IBM SPSS. Specifically, this expresses itself as the ever-growing acceptance of individuals into data science positions with limited software training and no experience in statistical theory, inference testing, and application. Many individuals who are familiar with some of the Big Data tools, and have taken a course or two in statistics (or none at all) are incorrectly deemed *data scientists* in the corporate world. Reviewing online data scientist job postings underscores this misconception.

Machine learning, although not a new concept or expression, is another current catchphrase in the analytic space. The basic tenet of machine learning is having computers "learn" on their own. There is clearly human involvement in creating the "learning" algorithms, but is limited to no intervention once these algorithms are initiated. Here again we have the idea of a "machine" doing the "thinking," obviating reliance on problem solving or critical thinking. Recently, there have been great strides in some machine learning[1] algorithms, especially a computer's ability to identify objects in images. These algorithms are extremely sophisticated and have impressive recognition and categorization capabilities. Are they going to pass a Turing (1950) test? We think that this is doubtful.

Big Data, machine learning, and the powerful array of analytical software tools in and beyond these domains are extremely powerful in helping us understand, analyze, and improve the world around us. These tools are not the solution. They are simply powerful aids to our thinking and not a replacement for the imagination, creativity, and critical reasoning skills of the human element.

Many organizations have invested millions of dollars in powerful software and hardware infrastructures but have not realized the full—or in many cases even partial—potential of these investments due to poorly trained employees with limited problem-solving skills. This disconnect and investment loss often lead to internal turmoil as well as external difficulties, sometimes culminating in legal battles with large software and hardware vendors being pursued by highly dissatisfied clients. Companies need to do a much better job of having the appropriate personnel in place to fully utilize sophisticated analytics capabilities and identify potential uses of analytics. The vendors who help install these capabilities also have to place much greater emphasis on ensuring that their clients have well-trained problem solvers on staff; if not, they need to offer more in-depth and longer training both onsite and online. Correcting the course, on both the client and vendor sides, will result in far fewer lost opportunities for both parties.

Academia

We estimated from our 2014 survey/interviews of analytics master's programs (Gorman & Klimberg, 2014) the topics covered and their percentage coverage was about:

- 50% statistical topics (basic statistics, regression, data mining, decision trees, neural nets)
- 25% OR topics (linear programming, simulation)
- 20% IT topics (database, programming, data warehousing)
- 5% mostly various business skills (communication, leadership)

The analytics courses in these programs focused on learning analytical techniques (such as decision trees, logistic regression, text mining, optimization, and simulation) and utilizing the analytical tools. In terms of software used, special educationally designed software was not used at any of the institutions. All the programs used Microsoft Office products. Professional software from each analytics' component area was used.

- IT: Oracle, Tableau, Cognos, SAP
- Statistics: SAS, JMP, Enterprise Miner, JMP, IBM/SPSS, Modeler
- OR: AMPL/CPLEX, Lindo, Arena

In addition, open-source programs such as Hadoop, R, and Python were used.

A brief examination of the current 145 MS analytics programs found a similar emphasis on analytic techniques and software employed.

A main concentration of these analytics courses is to provide the students with a sufficient introduction to the analytics tools, techniques, and technology. In these courses, a technique or tool is taught, and the students are subsequently given a homework assignment and/or a case assignment. The primary objective of these assignments is to see if the students follow/ understood what is presented. With both assignments, the professors already "gave away the house!" The students know the assignment requires them to use the technique/tool just covered in class. The students perform fairly well on these assignments. However, when it comes to the end-of-semester final exam that covers all (or most) of the techniques/tools in the course, many students have difficulty deciding which technique/tool is the appropriate technique/tool to use. Further evidence arises in subsequent courses, when covering a topic in which a previously learned technique is applicable to the situation. Students either do not make the connection, do not remember, or even worse: try to use a learned technique inappropriately. Students are exposed to numerous techniques, tools, and technology, yet their overall problem-solving skills are poor and not sufficiently developed.

Lack of development of problem-solving skills is not isolated to analytics programs. Quantitative/math skills are not properly developed, and it is widespread from grade school to higher education. For example, in business schools:

Although business schools teach how swiftly the business environment is changing, instruction in quantitative methods has barely changed in almost half a century... generally faculty resist increasing the quantitative literacy of business students because they believe that (a) all business students do not need much mathematics beyond the high school level except for a course in statistics and (b) calculus is an unnecessary hurdle. "I've never used calculus in all these years" is a common refrain.... This reluctance to increase the emphasis on quantitative literacy has resulted in it being practically nonexistent in business curricula. (McClure & Sircar, 2008)

Overall, the problem-solving skills of U.S. students are well below the average of industrialized nations (Dobbs, 2004a, 2004b). A recent study conducted by the Education Testing Service (ETS) of Millennials (born after 1980) from 22 industrialized countries showed U.S. Millennials tied for last in both problem-solving and math skills (Sparks, 2015).

Problem-solving skills can be broken down into four components:

1. Realization: Given a problem situation realizing that an analytic model could solve the problem
2. Abstraction: Given a problem situation, understanding and identifying the relevant variables and their roles (independent versus dependent variables, controllable versus uncontrollable variables); conceptualize, structure, and develop an abstract representation of the problem situation
3. Selection: Determining which analytics techniques are or are not appropriate to solve the problem situation
4. Development and execution: Develop the model and get it running in some analytics software package (including Excel).

The major focus of these technique/tool analytics classes is on the development and execution component. Students formulate an optimization model, produce a simulation model, or create a statistical model. They evaluate their model—if relevant evaluate it statistically—or examine the model's sensitivity or validate its results. Additionally, students may present their results, either orally or in a written report.

The other three problem-solving components are to varying degrees only briefly examined in these courses.

To address the realization problem-solving component, some introductory class discussion examines different examples of applications of the techniques and tools to demonstrate their diversity, with discussions on where and when to use them.

Students learn the methodologies to apply the techniques and tools; yet, little time is spent on developing the necessary modeling strategies to determine the appropriate techniques/tools to solve an unknown problem situation, i.e., little to no time is devoted to the development of the problem-solving skills of abstraction and selection. In the classroom problems, all the data presented is relevant to most of the situations addressed. Given a new/unknown problem situation, students are unable to appreciate or identify the full value of the hints and operators to provide direction to a possible solution to the problem. Students tend to work from familiar formulas and available variables, and not to model the problem and its behaviors. They have difficulty getting and interpreting a "bird's-eye view."

An analogy is that we teach students how to use a hammer, drill, saw, and other tools; yet, they don't know anything about how to be a carpenter. That is, given a stack of lumber and other building materials, they have no idea how to start building a house. We need to teach the abstraction and selection problem-solving skills or the craft of modeling skills so the students can become master carpenters. The craft of modeling skills of problem solving is the "Holy Grail" of problem-solving skills (Klimberg & McCullough, 2013). It is the most difficult to teach and to learn, yet it is so crucial.

The development of a *modeling science* to teaching modeling was called for in the CONDOR Report (1988). However, "The teaching of models is not equivalent to the teaching of modeling" (Morris, 1967). The craft of modeling needs to be taught. For example, in an art of modeling course, Powell emphasizes the craft of modeling and improves the match between the decision maker (student) and the problem-solving task. The problem-solving tool that Powell expects his students, who are MBA students, to use to "solve" and to represent the problem is a spreadsheet (Powell, 1995a, 1995b). The students learn to develop heuristics to gain insights and the skills to analyze practical problem situations. The application of heuristics is one of the fundamental problem-solving strategies employed by expert modelers (Schön, 1983).

Another illustration to teach modeling skills is one of the numerous competitions/challenges offered by schools (Manhattan College Analytics Competition and Conference; Iowa MBA Business Analytics Case Competition), software companies (SAS-2016 Analytics Shootout; Tableau-NIC Face-off) or analytics groups (Kaggle; Teradata University Network (TUN) Data Challenge; INFORMS O.R., & Analytics Student Team Competition).

ANALYTICAL GRAND ROUNDS (AGR)

The skills to analyze a problem situation and build a model are fundamental skills taught to physicians. Physicians demonstrate their problem-solving skills in diagnosing, prescribing, testing, and determining courses of action.

Physicians are taught to both inculcate and regularly demonstrate problem-solving skills in the practice of medicine through a protocol called SOAP (subjective, objective, assessment, and plan). In the *subjective* phase, the patient describes the problem to the physician (the reason for their visit). In the *objective* phase, the physician conducts objective tests (e.g., x-ray, EKG, CBC, etc.) that employ observation and analytics to assess outcomes. Based on the patient's complaints and test results derived from clinical data and analytics, the physician makes an *assessment* (diagnosis) leading to a *plan* of action (more tests, prescriptions, nothing, etc.). Physicians develop and apply heuristics to improve and sharpen their problem-solving skills. Formalized heuristics (or protocols) help to articulate the logic of a process and its relevance to the problem under scrutiny. In effect, a decision-making protocol such as SOAP provides functional context and legitimacy for the analytics employed, enabling them to be made clearly relevant to the goals of the decision-making process.

Grand rounds are an integral part of a physician's medical education and continuing education. Physicians are presented with the medical situation of a particular patient. In an effort to constructively critique the physician's decision making that's relative to patient care the possible alternative diagnoses, tests, and treatments are considered and discussed. As a result of these sessions, a physician's clinical problem-solving skills are enhanced.

Similar to medical education, analytics programs need to have as a primary part of their program an analytics grand rounds (AGR) course and other similar exposures to develop students' analytics heuristics skills.

An AGR course would require bringing real-world problems into the classroom. The aforementioned analytics competitions/challenges certainly provide the students with wonderful opportunities. These experiences are examples of what is called experiential learning (EL). EL is the process of learning by doing. These experiences do significantly improve students' modeling skills. However, a true EL experience should not be completely focused on the product of learning, such as in these competitions, but should be directed toward the process of learning. A significant added step in an AGR course needs to take the EL experience to this next level: to have students exposed to, discussing, and critiquing several other problem situations. This added step would enhance their problem-solving skills significantly.

For example, we used real-world data for medical and pharmaceutical claims, and combined a pharmaceutical marketing and an analytics class (Sillup, Klimberg, & McSweeney, 2010). In a collaborative process to mimic how the pharmaceutical industry works, each integrated student team was to determine the potential of a new drug. They worked together and taught each other their respective knowledge areas, e.g., marketing and analytics. Throughout the course, teams interacted by presenting, critiquing, and providing suggestions. This collaborative learning experience worked well. The students not only experienced an increase understanding of another discipline, but more so, they developed a much deeper understanding of their own discipline.

The AGR course should expose students to numerous problem situations in which we do not "give away the house." That is, there should be discussions of possible technique/tool solutions and critiques of each approach.

This additional step should not be limited to one practicum AGR course. It should prevail throughout the analytics program. For example:

- In analytics techniques/tools courses, professors should present their own and/or bring in guest speakers, to discuss their real-world experiences employing a technique. These presentations should not only focus on the final end product, but also on the selection, development, and implementation of the model.
- Each analytics techniques/tools course should not be discrete; that is, the applicability of previously taught techniques/tools should be discussed and developed.
- The craft of modeling and the development and application of analytical heuristics should be developed throughout the program.
- The analytics program should have a computer programming course in which the students not only learn the programming language, but are required to develop programs for different problem situations.
- If logistics of program delivery make it possible, students should provide analytics support and tutoring—quite similar to a physician's residency—to students in lower level analytics classes.

CONCLUSIONS

Within most organizations, the use of and importance of analytics has been and will be increasing. At the same time, the number of lost opportunities (i.e., the number of misuses of analytics or the inability to recognize the opportunity to use analytics) is growing. A major reason for these lost opportunities is that the academic analytics programs poorly develop students' problem-solving skills. The students are learning the latest analytics techniques and tools, but their problem-solving skills are so poor they do not know when or where to use these techniques and tools. Analytics academic programs need to adjust and add as a primary focus of their programs the development of students' problem-solving skills. In this paper, we suggest a way to accomplish this improvement in problem-solving skills is to follow the education model of physicians, in which problem-solving is emphasized throughout a program.

Not all doctors are preeminent diagnosticians or experts in certain specialties, such as particular types of surgery. Similarly, not all analytics professionals will excel at problem solving. We recommend that organizations not hire solely experts in techniques or tools, but have a core group of analytics professionals who are unsurpassed at problem solving. As a result, the number of opportunities lost will be minimized.

NOTE

1. Although beyond the scope of this paper, there is great overlap between machine learning and computational statistics. Many core concepts from machine learning are directly lifted from statistical procedures that were formulated decades (or more) prior, including statistical techniques originating from the general linear model (GLM), such as regression, cluster and factor analysis, and the exploratory vs. confirmatory, supervised vs. unsupervised, and data mining aspects of GLM techniques. The machine learning domain considers neural networks, decision trees, optimization algorithms, and a host of Bayesian procedures as falling under their umbrella as well.

REFERENCES

Anderson, C. (2008, June 23). The end of theory: The data deluge makes the scientific method obsolete. *Wired* Magazine.

Committee on the Next Decade in Operations Research (CONDOR). (1988, July/August). Operations research: The next decade. *Operations Research, 36*(4), 619–637.

Connolly, J. M. (2016, August). *Take analytics education beyond the tools.* http://www.allanalytics.com/author.asp?section_id=3624&doc_id=281176&f_src=allanalytics_sitedefault&elqTrackId=d78a7744e37b49d09f0f4c59c0a4941b&elq=2b5cd5d9b8ca45b9add9de7f29fa928d&elqaid=71882&elqat=1&elqCampaignId=22461

Dobbs, M. (2004a, December 7). In a global test of math skills, U.S. students behind the curve. *The Washington Post.*

Dobbs, M. (2004b, December 1). Good news, bad news about U.S. students released. *The Washington Post.*

Gorman, M. F., & Klimberg, R. K. (2014, May/June). Benchmarking academic programs in business analytics. *Interfaces, 44*(3), 329–341.

Grossman, T. A. (2002, December). The keys to the vault. *OR/MS Today, 20*(6), 12–13.

INFORMS. (2013). *Home page.* Retrieved from https://www.informs.org/Community/Analytics

Klimberg, R., & McCullough, B. D. (2013). Business analytics: Today's green? *Contemporary Perspectives in Data Mining, 1*(1), 47–60.

Manyika, J. M., Chui, B., Brown, J., Bughin, R., Dobbs, C., Roxburgh, A., & Hung, B. (2011, May). *Big data: The next frontier for innovation, competition and productivity.* Retrieved from http://www.mckinsey.com/business-functions/digital-mckinsey/our-insights/big-data-the-next-frontier-for-innovation

Master's in Data Science. (2016, September). *Business analytics master's degrees.* Retrieved from http://www.mastersindatascience.org/specialties/business-analytics/

McClure, R., & Sircar, S. (2008, July/August). Quantitative literacy for undergraduate business students in the 21st century. *Journal of Education for Business, 83*(6), 369–374.

Morris, W. (1967). On the art of modeling. *Management Science, 13*, B707–B717.

Powell, S. G. (1995a). Teaching the art of modeling to MBA students. *Interfaces, 25*(3), 88–94.

Powell, S. G. (1995b). Six key modeling heuristics. *Interfaces, 25*(4), 114–125.

Powell, S. G. (2001). Teaching modeling in management science. *INFORMS Transactions on Education, 1,* 2.

Renzulli, K. A., Weisser, C., & Leonhardt, M. (2016, May 16). *The 21 most valuable career skills now.* Retrieved from http://time.com/money/4328180/most-valuable-career-skills/

Schön, D. R. (1983). *The reflective practitioner: How professionals think in action.* New York, NY: Basic Books.

Sillup, G., Klimberg, R., & McSweeney, D. P. (2010, March). Data-driven decision making for new drugs: A collaborative learning experience. *International Journal of Business Intelligence Research.* doi: 10.4018/jbir.2010040105

Silver, Nate (2012). *The signal and the noise: Why so many predictions fail—but some don't.* New York, NY: Penguin Press.

Sparks, S. D. (2015, February 17). U.S. millennials come up short in global skills study. http://www.edweek.org/ew/articles/2015/02/18/us-millennials-come-up-short-in-global.html

Turing, A. (1950). Computing machinery and intelligence. *Mind, 59*(236), 433–460.

ABOUT THE EDITORS

Dr. Kenneth D. Lawrence is a Professor of Management Science and Business Analytics in the School of Management at the New Jersey Institute of Technology. Professor Lawrence's research is in the areas of applied management science, data mining, forecasting, and multi-criteria decision-making. His current research works include multi-criteria mathematical programming models for productivity analysis, discriminant analysis, portfolio modeling, quantitative finance, and forecasting/data mining. He is a full member of the Graduate Doctoral Faculty of Management at Rutgers, The State University of New Jersey in the Department of Management Science and Information Systems and a Research Fellow in the Center for Supply Chain Management in the Rutgers Business School. His research work has been cited over 1,750 times in over 235 journals, including: *Computers and Operations Research, International Journal of Forecasting, Journal of Marketing, Sloan Management Review, Management Science,* and *Technometrics.* He has 375 publications in 28 journals including: *European Journal of Operational Research, Computers and Operations Research, Operational Research Quarterly, International Journal of Forecasting* and *Technometrics.* Professor Lawrence is associated editor of the *International Journal of Strategic Decision Making* (IGI Publishing). He is also associated editor of the *Review of Quantitative Finance and Accounting* (Springer Verlag), as well as associate editor of the *Journal of Statistical Computation and Simulation* (Taylor and Francis). He is editor of *Advances in Business and Management Forecasting* (Emerald Press), editor of *Applications of Management Science* (Emerald Press), and editor of *Advances in Mathematical Programming and Financial Planning* (Emerald Press).

Contemporary Perspectives on Data Mining, Volume 3, pages 161–162
Copyright © 2018 by Information Age Publishing

Dr. Ronald K. Klimberg, is a professor in the Department of Decision Systems Sciences of the Haub School of Business at Saint Joseph's University. Dr. Klimberg has published 3 books, including his *Fundamentals of Predictive Analytics Using JMP*, edited 9 books, over 50 articles and made over 70 presentations at national and international conferences. His current major interest include multiple criteria decision making (MCDM), multiple objective linear programming (MOLP), data envelopment analysis (DEA), facility location, data visualization, data mining, risk analysis, workforce scheduling, and modeling in generation. He is currently a member of INFORMS, DSI, and MCDM. Ron was the 2007 recipients of the Tenglemann Award for his excellence in scholarship, teaching, and research.

Printed in the United States
By Bookmasters